To Joanne + Nord
God Bless and
thank you for your
support. Deborah ...

God Bless you
& thanks for you
Kara Wil...
8-1-98

Joe Ann
What a wonderful
Surprise to see you
Feels Good
"God's Blessings"
Hans Metayer

Thank you
Joanne
God Bless!
Michael Simmons
8/1/98

Joann,
Thanks for
the support
and enjoy the
book —
Gerri Metayer
"H"

To Joanne
My best to you
always...
Al Ward

To Joanne
God Bless
& thank you
for your
support.
Dianne Rhodes
'98

To Joanne
I hope you
enjoy "Paradise Lost"
and "Ms. Maggie Smith".
Joyce Cade-Hilton
8-1-98

To Joanne
thanks for your
support! Heather ...

MW01658283

PARADISE VALLEY DAYS

A Photo Album Poetry Book of Black Detroit, 1930's to 1950's

By

The Detroit Black Writer's Guild

Paradise Valley Days
A Photo Album Poetry Book of Black Detroit 1930's to 1950's

ISBN 1-888754-02-8
Library of Congress Catalog Card Number: 97-078432

Detroit Black Writer's Guild, Inc.
5601 West Warren
Detroit, MI 48210

Cover Art Design by Herbert R. Metoyer

The Detroit Black Writer's Guild is a non-profit literary organization. Its primary goals are to improve literacy awareness, train & encourage aspiring authors, preserve Black Heritage, and serve as a publishing platform for ethnic literature.

Funding for this project was furnished, in part, by a Grant from the Michigan Council For Arts and Cultural Affairs

mc aca michigan council for arts and cultural affairs

Printed in the United States of America

DEDICATION

This book is respectfully dedicated to —

Mrs. Peggy A. Moore, Matriarch and Founder of The Detroit Black Writer's Guild. This book, one of her life-long goals, was initiated by her four years ago. It is regretful that she is not here to see it finally completed.

and to...
Reginald Larrie, Michigan Chronicle, one of our benefactors — A quiet person who devoted his life to promoting "Black History" through words and deeds....

and to...
Geraldine Williams Metoyer, the wife of our Executive Director, for understanding and tolerating our passion for the Guild....

Heather Buchanan
Chairperson, Board of Directors

Farewell

Farewell, my Dear, Dear Friend.
May God speed you on your way.
Keep warm, travel light,
and do not be concerned for us.
And when you reach that distant shore,
build you a large fire,
One that I may see from a great distance
so that I may find you easily.
And there on the banks
of the River Jordan,
We will sit and speak of times past,
and those yet to come.
Of what was, and what was not,
and what could have been,
Of what is, and what is not,
and what should have been.
We shall read each other's prose,
and listen to each other's yarns.
And in the evenings, we will follow the sun
to the place where we can hear
The laughter of the children
you loved so well.
But until that time,
or until the coming of the one who is coming,
rest easy in the bosom of God's Love
Knowing that you —
will be truly missed.....

PEGGY A. MOORE
FOUNDER, DETROIT BLACK WRITER'S GUILD
1932 – 1997

Herbert R. Metoyer, Jr. July 1997

INTRODUCTION TO PARADISE VALLEY DAYS—

A time most commonly referred to as the — *Renaissance*, a clever expression used to de scribe a struggling people's efforts to find their identity in the decaying rubble and debris left behind by the Reconstruction era. An era that had promised everything but gave nothing.

A time when a people dug up their roots, packed shoe boxes filled with funky day-old chicken, bread, and sweet potatoes; and left the peanut, cotton, and cane fields of the South. Climbing aboard loose-fendered trucks, or into the crowded back seats of highway buses, or the crowded front seats of sweat-box railway coaches, they headed north to exotic places like New York, St. Louis, Chicago, and Detroit — searching for the land of milk and honey — *Paradise.*

Many of these wayfarers found their way to Detroit where they gained some token of economic growth by working in the automobile factories, in Caucasian homes and hotels as domestics, or as train porters. The majority of them lived acquiescently, crowded into a small section of the downtown area often referred to as the "*Black Bottom*."

In this climate, however, Black businesses began to take root. As the Jewish population migrated out of the Inner City, the black community and businesses expanded in their wake. And while we are on the subject, that of glancing back at our past, let us not forget the role the Jewish people played in providing economic assistance to Black Americans. Despite some of the things we hear today, there was a time when the Jewish nation and the Black race enjoyed a mutually amicable association. I, for one, can attest to this fact. For even in Louisiana, if it had not been for the Jewish family who financed and assisted my father to get his first business started, my family would probably still be struggling to survive. My father had a third grade education and no property for collateral. Fortunately, his business thrived and he was able to see that his wife and seven children received a college education.

When we, the Guild, started this project, it was not our intent to produce a text book compiled from extensive research. We leave that task to the more qualified experts in the field. Our purpose was to:

1 — Produce a poetry book.
2 — Increase public awareness of a past era in Detroit's Black history.
3 — Collect and preserve old photographs for future posterity, and...
4 — To educate, so that we can learn to appreciate, preserve and protect who we are and what we have in hand. Maybe then, we will not make the same mistakes again.

Because we did not want to limit our scope only to the official boundaries of "Paradise Valley," we chose the title, "*Paradise Valley Days*." This title, we felt, embraced an "era" or a "time," as opposed to a specific place. It also allowed us to explore or ramble throughout the city in our search for artifacts. During our crusade, we encountered people who were quite eager to share their photographic treasures, and we also ran into a few who declined to share at this time. I sincerely hope, however, that eventually these valuable items will someday find their way into some *reference* publication or into the *Burton Historical Library* for the benefit of future generations and researchers in the field of urban renewal.

The photographs that are included in this book were selected for their thought provoking and nostalgic qualities. In many cases, we were unable to identify the subjects. This, however, does not detract from their value. Each old photograph tells its own unique story while at the same time forces us to recognize how vulnerable we are to the ravages of time. As we speculate about the lives of each subject, hopefully, we will find ourselves speculating about our own lives—a process that could be beneficial to our future growth.

And so, to the City of Detroit and the State of Michigan, we, the Detroit Black Writer's Guild, humbly present to you this poetic work and collection of mementos from a small segment of our history, hoping that you will embrace this book with as much affection as the staff responsible for its creation....

Herbert R. Metoyer, Jr.
Executive Director & Executive Editor

PARADISE VALLEY

by

Peggy A. Moore

In its heyday, back in the 1940's, 50's, and 60's, Paradise Valley, a Black Mecca that was located on the lower east side of Detroit, dazzled and attracted more weekend visitors to her door step than did Greek Town or China Town during the same period.

Paradise Valley came of age during the height of segregation in Detroit. Legal "Deed Restrictions" prohibited a Negro from renting or owning property in all but the most wretched parts of the city — all on the lower east side. Back then, a Negro could be thrown in jail for being caught in any area west of Woodward Avenue.

It was in this climate that Negro businessmen like Charles Roxbourgh, Irvine Rhone, John White, and others took a somewhat condemned area bounded by Gratiot, Vernor, Brush, and Hastings and carved out "Paradise Valley."

At that time, Negroes had no political power. No one that looked like them was allowed to sit in the mayor's office or hold a seat on the "Common Council." For this reason, the citizens of Paradise Valley got together, erected their own City Hall, and elected Roy Lightfoot as their first mayor.

Did you know that before integration came to Detroit, Paradise Valley actually had more Negroes in business than any other city in the country?

This was due largely to the fact that Negroes who worked for the automobile industry earned fairly decent wages and they had a lot of money to spend. There were also many Railroad Porters who called Detroit their home, and they, too, were well paid.

As a result, businesses flourished. On St. Antoine Street there was Watson' Realty Co., Donald F. White Architect, Long's Cut-Rate Drug Store, Law Offices of Lewis-Rowlette-Brown; Biddy's Chicken Shack; Wilson's Modern Laundry; Wayne County Better Homes; Pekin Restaurant; Biltmore Hotel; Modern Barber Shop; The Pryor Hotel, and many others. By the way, most of the businesses used Richard Austin, who later became Secretary of State for Michigan, as their accountant.

All of these businesses were solvent, meaning that they operated profitably. And while all black businesses had to put their money in white-owned banks, none of the banks in the city at that time would hire a black in any position except that of a janitor.

On weekends, especially during the summer months, taxis ran almost non-stop between the train and bus stations transporting travellers and visitors into the city. Some to visit friends and family, and others who came just to relax and have a *good time*. A great majority of the visitors came from the south to get a taste of big city life.

At night, cocktail lounges, dance halls, showbars, and restaurants all came alive with dazzling lights, swing bands, sultry singers, dancers doing the *Black Bottom, Jitterbub,* or *Hulley Gulley*, and jazz and blues artist all on center stage. It was a time for "*Zoot Suits*," long watch chains, and wide brimmed Stetson hats.

In many ways, Paradise Valley was not unlike Harlem in New York. No Negro musician worth the *salt in his bread* would ever think of coming to Detroit City without visiting the "Valley." And it was there that you would find giants like Duke Ellington, Jimmy Lunceford, Lionel Hampton, Fats Waller, Cab Calloway, McKinney's Cotton Pickers, Louis Armstrong, and all the other Hep Cats....

URBAN RENEWAL LANDS

FOR SALE

COMMERCIAL PARCELS

FOR INFORMATION

CALL WO. 30955

DETROIT HOUSING COMMISSION

PERHAPS YOU'D LIKE TO BUY IT BACK

TABLE OF CONTENTS

Genesis

While small fires blaze
and strangers gather to share
its warmth and space
I think of the road behind
and the distance traveled
to reach this place
Of the lineage left behind
lost forever
without a trace
Silently, I listen
as they speak of times,
ancient, and places, rare
And I am stricken
with the fever
For I long to visit there

The smoldering fire
soon loses it brilliance
Friends now part
to go their separate way
Circling the circled circle
each prompted
in a programmed way
to follow the retreating
horizon,
to search each blessed day
for that silent, mystic land
so far,
far away....

Paradise Valley Remembered

Like an unassuming lady
abducted and vaguely abject
She stands at the crossroads of the city;
wheedling winds attack her back
And on her cold shoulders
chattering brown birds and gulls relax.
Unblinking — like a peculiar marble statue
she's bathed in soft velvets of twilight
Winking street lights splash colors rhythmically
on roofs of speeding vehicles on the go.
And on damp asphalt her sober, expressionless face
seems to assume an asorbing glow.
Her fiber, capricious breezes cannot whisk away,
like submissive leaves that fall at her feet and soon decay.
Her spirit struggles through broken branches and objectively hovers
over the wild flowers that dress her jagged pathway.
Gilded messages scribbled on her crumbling walls
render lucid clues and hints
of the essence of her yolk
belated... and bemused.

SECTION I — THE JOURNEY

Submitted by Peggy A. Moore

Southern Road

(for Obirtha & Argentry Williams)

I never knew
the south of my parents
or their parents
or their parents or...
the Africa that preceded that
I never knew their sun,
their hot,
it's warmth
much different than that
filtered by the northern lights now
their sky dark
full of stars
unseen by me most of my life
little patches of green
little patches borrowed from
their mutual memories
trying to recreate a safe haven
for them and the eight of us
behind our houses
transplanted gardens of Eden
for transplanted folks from the land
longing for a home, longing for freedom.

COLORED DETROIT

Mildred Winder -*Submitted by Sandra Miller*

Emma Harris & Children George & Dora

Submitted by Geraldine Metoyer

Paradise Lost

The neighborhood is old
as brown as I am
cold where the wind
wraps its ugly white breath around time-bitten trees
pushing their essence down into soil
around the bittersweet cracks of rot-gut on stilts
somebody has the audacity to live in
and in some places, warm as neighbors houses
dressed in the fat pillow albums of print-dressed
elders,
echoes of schools and families that have seen their
renaissance.
brick brownstones once wrapped in pink cotton
candy
in some yards an even odder pink fence.
Long ago, smiling-lipped children scouring the streets
looking for dimes, nickles, pennies
an ashy-kneed sweetheart to spend them on
the penny candy lady and her mountain of sweets
No need to warn of ills of the needle
pending destruction, the rum-spiced eyes and hands
of the neighborhood addict looking thin, around
corners
for a slim-hipped fix. People like him, are the children
now,
the essence of life bleeding in code blue rhythms
the force of tears sliding down the back of the throat.

© 1997 Karen Williams

Mildred Winder - *Submitted by Sandra Miller*

Courtesy of Jacqueline Caffey Collection

Library of Congress

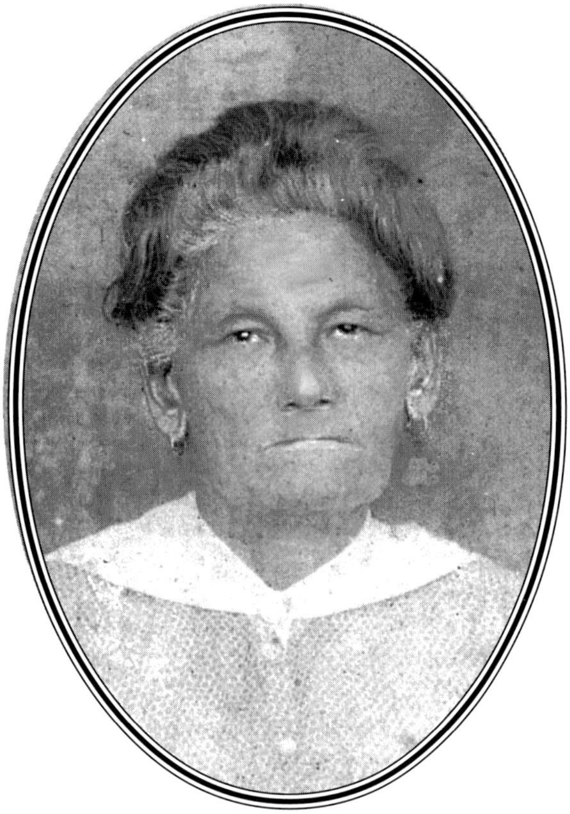

Submitted by Geraldine Metoyer

Courtesy of Jacqueline Caffey Collection

Dora Thomas *Submitted by Geraldine Metoyer*

DETROIT CONTENDER

Courtesy of Jacqueline Caffey Collection

Samuel Quinney (seated). L to R, Daughter, Leanna & wife, Mariah *- Courtesy of Jewel Martin*

Jewel Martin & Father, Samuel Quinney, Jr. - *Courtesy of Jewel Martin*

Charlie Mae Daniel - *Courtesy of Jewel Martin*

Charlie Mae Daniel - *Courtesy Of Jewel Martin*

Detroit-Chicago Train Time

Michigan Central railroad station,
ancient Greek temple
Doric columns
Corinthian cloisters.
The walls and floors could sing
had they voices.

World War II troop trains
from all over the country,
stopping for a moment
at Michigan Central.

From the station to the train yard
reminds you
Frankfurt, 1944-45.
Twisted pieces of concrete and
steel
like black and red licorice.

Yards of junk,
pieces of brown-green
machinery
Houses that sit and look at you
through dirty windows.
Yards back and front
stuffed full of cots, chairs,
ovens, refrigerators.
Yes, a portable swimming pool.

Fields of corn, some cabbage,
cows slapping air in search of
flies,
horses ogling grass
19th century railroad stations
Niles, Kalamazoo, Jackson.

My friend and colleague, Cleo
Harpoon,
working her treatise
"The History of Junk,"
might find this route ideal
for a museum
of everything nobody wants.

Selection from "Watermelon Seeds & Cherry Pits," Broadside Press

Courtesy of Jacqueline Caffey Collection

Courtesy of Jacqueline Caffey Collection

—LaJune Rodgers, Age 12— The look in her eyes—tell all. *See her story on page 70.* *Courtesy of Virgil Rodgers Collection*

Nate Lawrence — *Submitted by Peggy A. Moore*

Liza Jane

To Detroit City
a young girl came,
Left her home in Georgia
on a north bound train,
What's her name?
Her name Little Liza,
Little Liza Jane.

Now River Rat Jack
was a cold, cold cat.
He gave little Liza
a tiny white pack,
Of cocaine.
Oh no, Little Liza,
Little Liza Jane.

Little Liza Jane
standing in the rain.
Waiting for her lover,
but he never came.
What's his game?
His game Little Liza,
Little Liza Jane.

Little Liza Jane
she couldn't stand the pain.
She died last winter
with an ounce of cocaine
Inside her veins.
Good bye, Little Liza,
Little Liza Jane.

Sweet orphaned baby
sweet as sugar cane.
Who is your mama,
who can we blame,
What's her name?
Her name Little Liza,
Little Liza Jane.

What-what. Wh... wh-what?
Her name Little Liza,
Little Liza Jane....
What-what.Wh... wh-what?
Her nam....

© 1987 Herbert & Michael Metoyer
(A Song Poem)

Ghetto's Morning Light

At twilight, morning sometimes
peeps
Curiously through the clouds.
Shimmering with rays
of sunshine
Unabashed and proud.

She wakes God's children,
his sleeping flowers,
From their cozy beds deep,
And banishes lingering shadows
of self-doubt
Where they dare to creep.

Her infancy dissolves
The inky armor of the dark,
Evoking peels of children's
laughter
That seduce stray dogs to bark.

She annoys homeless beggars
Shivering in cardboard boxes in
the dismantled park,
Revealing malicious messages on
crumbling walls
Where the uncelebrated artist
sprayed his disgusting mark!

© 1997 James Neal Ware

The Titanic & John Dan
The Shoeshine Man

This ship is headed for troubled
waters
Oh me, oh my
This ship is headed for troubled
waters
And I don't want to die

Fair sailing weather, someone
cried
When we sailed out to sea
Fair sailing weather, someone lied
Now it's plain to see.

Now we ride the angry sea
Each swell a fathom high
Each time we crest across the
top
I swear we touch the sky.

Lord, you took away my slaving
chains
Thank you for your support
Now help this ship to make dry
land
and get Ole John to port.

No one ever heard me say
That I did love the sea
I just came along to ride
Lord, please save po' me.

I don't want no water grave
Deep down in the sea
A six foot hole in the desert sand
Would do just fine for me.

Lord, please melt this big ice
cube
and lick this ocean dry
If not, then give me a pair of
wings
And teach Ole John to fly.

Lord, If I make it to dry land
Tell you what I'll do
I'll bury my anchor in the sand
And the other end to you.

© 1975 Herbert R. Metoyer

L & N
RAILROAD

Black-Velvet-Valley

Legend lives in Paradise Valley
beyond forgotten neon signs,
and tawdry streets
Like lithography gone wild
Hasting Street jumps alive to
dance with mystery

The world tastes
Black Bottom's strong booze,
and becomes high
from a quiet-dark-Camelot hour
nestled in a cozy corner of
power.

From four winds come
the sounds of mellow-jazz
litany against heart-wrenching
blues
where a dazzling strip
more than paid their dues
to a brewery and a parking lot.

Walleyed visionaries
turned not
their eyes from a silkened night
which barred
the iconoclasts
with all its might.

New Walleyes will see
the dam burst again
from Black Bottom
onto Paradise Valley
Without darkened pupils
visions of dark waters
will come in sight
and celebrate
legendary life

TRAILWAYS BUS COMPANY

Patches On Mainstreet

Not so old
but worn like his coat
he hangs to the side of life
made of brown patches,
pieces of string.

Up/down Woodward
arms hung low,
Patches leans
when he walks past
the downtown windows.
Street folk trust Patches.
He never turns away
when they ask...
"Patches, you got any quarters?"
"God don't like ugly,"
Patches'd say.
"Seen the best and worst
of all life's offerings,
I'll give you a hard time
if I think'yr hustling."

At Grand Circus Park,
the Pigeon lady feeds
her friends ...bits of corn,
her hands like white porcelain,
feet bound in old newspaper.
Her doll's head silent,
cotton hair tangled
with feathers,
a red scarf around her neck,
Patches would say
to anyone watching,
"She is innocent, Jesus loves her."

In Kennedy Square,
the cowboy dances.
Rights, lefts, jabs and crosses,
hooks, straights...He practices,
prances, shadow boxes.
Passersby shake their heads.
Some point, laugh, make com-
ment.
"Look at this fool in cowboy
boots
acting like he's a champion."
"I used to do this," Patches hears
between the cowboy's punches
"I used to do this."
The cowboy's words crack/
stumble.

Patches wears an old brown hat
where he keeps hope and
conversation.
Patches wears two shirts
and sometimes a sweater
beneath his grey tweed jacket.

Patches, not so old
but worn like his coat
hangs to the side of life
in his search for truth
with a shoestring
tied around his soul.

These Men

Made of brown paper
and rag cloths
...these men stand 'round
an oil barrel in a vacant lot
near a liquor store
"tellin' lies."
Casualties ...of living

These men had names once,
families, friends,
knew love, its loss,
dreamed, failed,
were forgotten
and never forgiven.

Scratched, rusted,
no longer useful
left discolored
without heritage or pension,
their world flat,
grey edged
with shadows and lies.....

these men.

Courtesy of The HildaVest Collection

Oswald & Leary Freeman - *Courtesy of The Hilda Vest Collection*

Hanna's Lament

When Hanna's little dark skinned child was born, Lou took one look, sat down, and cried like a baby. She cried, too. For days, he moped around, refusing to let her look into his eyes, leaving her to wonder if the shame he felt was directed at her or himself. Three weeks later, when he was certain that Collette was not his, he left, caught the Missouri Pacific for Detroit. Not one word of good-bye, just a hastily written note saying that he had borrowed the sixty dollars she had saved.

She never heard from Lou again.

For a long time, she had waited, hoping for his return. Sometimes, on especially lonely days, she would get up and walk clear across town to watch the train pull into the depot. And when the conductors and their stinking train had departed, she would stand in the middle of the tracks cursing, and wondering how many fucking fools it took to lay the many miles of hot, steel rails it took to run all the way up to Detroit and Chicago.

Nowadays, she didn't go near the station, and she cringed each time the wind carried the sound of their steam whistles to her side of town. How she hated railroad trains, the way they growled and frightened decent folks. She hated them too, for the effect they had on the little black boys who churned through the neighborhood, all in a line, playing choo-choo train, and dreaming hopeless dreams of becoming conductors, firemen, and engineers when all the best of them could ever hope to be was nothing but a shit-eating, ass-kissing porter. But most of all, she hated them because they took people faraway — to places like... Detroit and Chicago....

Excerpt from "Before I Wake," Detroit Black Writer's Guild

The Traveller

I once walked for miles,
down an endless dusty road,
seemingly without purpose,
in a kind of leisure mode.
Stopping on occasions,
from day to blessed day,
To visit the many taverns,
I found along the way.
To drink their sweet rum,
and sing their sad songs,
To wait upon the sunrise,
and the night to be gone.

Wild painted women,
dressed in naked colored skirts,
Danced upon my table,
then left me to hurt.
And when I thought I'd come
to my journey's end,
You entered majestically,
and I lived again.
At peace with the world,
and all things within.
Secure in a love,
existing without bounds,
Thankful for today,
and the joy I have found.....

Sharecroppers Dream

Toby, stop all that dreamin'
Here come da man
Last time he was here
Bubba talk'in like that
He went an got da klan

They made sure po' Bubba
Never talked bout freedom again
Hung him up dat tree down dair
Put his life to an end.

So, if you was smart
You'd keep your mouth shut
You just keep doin' what-cha
doin'
And follow your gut

One of des days,
Our day gon' come, you hear
But till then, don't do nuthin'
And don't shed one tear

Every night I kneel to pray
Dis is what I say
Lord please come and take me
Away from here someday

Hoping He'll lead me
North to Detroit City
Where I can raise my family
Buy stuff, dress up pretty

Where I can be free
Just as free as any bird
Where words like discrimination
Is seldom ever heard

Where I can get a job and work
At a trade that's all my own
Spend my money how I want to
Sho' folks I is grown

Where my kids can play
Without worrying about race or
color
Where folks is proud of what dey
is
One no better than the other
Where I can drink from the
fountain
Just like the whitest man
And if he messes with me
Go to court, make my stand

Then, I'll sing my song
Finally, I is free
Nobody to answer to
Nobody, but me
Nobody...
But me....

A Few Ways to Look At Cleo

You —
Daughter of the Soil
Tawny frame
Wearing golden crown
Of diamond, pearl,
Emerald, topaz
The Empire's
First in Command
Second to none
Queen of the Nile

You —
Daughter of the Soil
Caesar's Cyprian nymph
Anthony's flame
Nefertiti calls you sister
Goddess by design
Lover by fame
Queen of the Nile

You —
Daughter of the Soil
Bleached palm sways
To cool your crowned brow
Love-slaves fan
Commonness away
Academe canonize
Your Afric name
Queen of the Nile

You —
Daughter of the Soil
Ladies bow on invisible knee
To the Eastern Star
Good Empress, Royal Cairo
Lofty Princess choosing to exit
Aspic juice embraced
Your train enjoined
With 'Rabian Bird
Ever-for
Queen of the Nile

You —
Dark threat to noble Emperor
Span years into decades
Queen of the Nile
Daughter...
Of the Soil....

Sunset, Sunrise

The clouds separate
and the sun goes
down, down, down.
It's bright colors
twinkle in my eyes.
The still, dark night
comes quickly
With spots of silver light
shining above me.
As the darkness slowly slips away,
I stare into the deep space
Knowing beautiful nights
don't last forever
But the love for them
will always be there.

Some Streets In My City

The Country Club, Barthwell Drugs,
Canfield and Brush.
Largest ice cream cone in America
for five big ones, 5 Cents.
Membership open to all!
Listen Willie the Pimp and Cadillac Bill,
discussing ways to spot the man
in order to stay loose.

To live in the city is to be smart
and dumb among all things.
To roam the streets, un-scarred
not possible — alive but scarred.
Unfunny streets — funny people
sirens whistle the song of promise,
untutored but schooled to life
that lets them survive.

Games played in the streets
Three Card Molly, Georgia Skin
one huge Shell Game
That gets us all.

The color of streets change.
Are we swift enough to understand
before the hurt gets us?
Do we have time to check the Sanskirt?

Semi-hip street-wise hustlers
live in the city.
Don't even know their ass
from a manhole cover.

Baby Ray, my main man
His place, The Bamboo Room
Not very legal, lots of action.
One day, he left some thing's with a man
to help pay for my learning.

Selection From "Watermelon Rinds & Cherry Pits" Broadside Press

Hastings Street

Much
earlier in this Century
say 1930 or thereabouts
was a place called Hastings
on the east side of Detroit.
Fact was,
way back then,
it was the only place
a black man could live
and really be deemed a man.
He
could open a business on Hastings,
A hospital,
call it the "Trinity"
and practice medicine
Or
a string of hotels and night spots;
a grocery store; a cleaners; a pool hall
Why...
he could create his very
own lottery system,
name it "The Policy"
and become rich overnight
He
could celebrate,
dance in the street
after each and every
Joe Louis win...
with all of his kin
on Hastings Street.
Pity
that place is long gone
now
not even a marker
"In memory of"
the sweet, sweet sounds
of her birth
her youth
of her demise....

SECTION II — THEIR DESTINATION

Hasting Street — as it appeared in 1910 when the area was predominately occupied by Jews. As they moved out, they sold their homes and businesses to blacks. They also financed or assisted many blacks in opening their own businesses.

Burton Historical Library

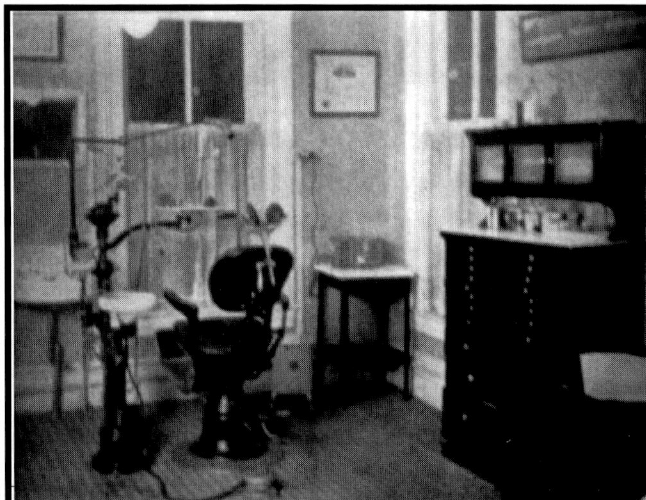

A Colored Dentist Office *Burton Historical Library*

Hasting Street — in 1961 *Burton Historical Library*

Paradise Theater — Buy a ticket & stay all night
Burton Historical Library

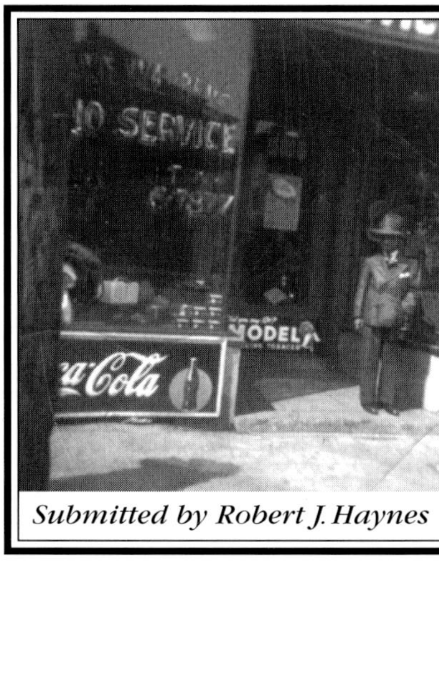

Submitted by Robert J. Haynes

Dudley Randall

Pushed through a crack in the
earth your eyes burn fire
Soft as soft your vision of cities:
GreenApples,
Roses and Revolution.
You find the green moss
discover north
tie square knots to hold our
world together
press the pressure points
to keep us from bleeding on city
streets.

In Paradise Valley,
your man Caruso flashes the
ruby stick-pin,
stands on his chair
talks about being colored.
Prophet Jones
sashays to his temple on Hague
floats to the pulpit
in his ermine robe
hands outstretched for alms.

Casablanca shadows
Orchestra Place,
touts his basement palace,
a place to look at cards,
have a taste or two.
You catch
the mellow harmony of their
beat
siphon time, bottle it,
then uncork
and stick it in our eye.

© 1991 Murray Jackson
Selection from "Watermelon Rinds & Cherry Pits," Broadside Press

Cherry 1623
McCullough
&
Jackson
Lawyers

Ad from Detroit Contender

Poem For An Old Man Sleeping In Old Paradise

Your eyes are thin, crusted,
a dull yellow
clinging to the curb of Madison
and St.Antoine,
the blur of roaring cars and
buses,
tuberculars coughing spume to
darken you
huddled in shadows of rust,
abandoned stores
to warm the threadbare blanket
you lie under,
clutch in fits until the men in
crisp white
come to cart you away
you, old friend of the Valley,
comrade of cigarettes,
the Senior Citizen's Smoke Shop,
the Horsehoe 606 with its wide-
thighed women
in painted lips and dresses
where are your dreams,
the hands that washed
and fed you,
that gave you no reason to drink,
to lay in your waste
and shudder your way
to the bottom of a withering
urban renewal
fed by a gambler's lust,
lurid fire-bombs of hate,
hands which fought a roach-
clipped desire
to preserve in the stench of
Thunderbird
the most pregnant of now opiate
memories:
the hot, safe bowls of salt pork
and crowder peas
your old woman's fragrance, the
scent of her cornmeal-fried fish
floating top-heavy in the clouds,
in the loud, proud music of your
talking sweet
to ladies to a *"Say there, Pretty
Lady? why don't you and me..."*
tune
Old friend of the Valley
who will heal your
crumbling curb,
the many lives raging
beneath its scars?

© 1997 Karen Williams

Bag Woman

These are my bags
I carry my dreams
My hatred, my nightmares
Stuffed and folded
Stacked, and twisted, and
crushed.
My bags are my fate
Holding dreams upon dreams
Defeat, honor, and love stuffed in
between.

A bag of dreams dragged upon
my feet
Buffed up, then layered down
Beaten slowly
Smoothed swiftly.

A bag of love held close to my
heart
Crushed, torn into bits
Wet with tears
With fragments of kisses
Touches of love
Soft glances
Unforgiving and cheated.

A bag for the nighttime
Full of fear
Loneliness and hunger
A remembrance of your smile
To be needed, shared, and loved.
Their heaviness covers my soul
They guide my destiny
They will never leave me
But you did....

© 1994 Evelyn L. Rhodes. Selection from "InnerVisions" Detroit Black Writer's Guild

God's Love
to you!
Evelyn L. Rhodes

Courtesy of Orlin Jones Collection

Paradise Valley

Milton's Paradise Valley
might have been lost
But, every soul I know found
joy and happiness in the
Valley
Would be Kings, Queens,
Barons and Dukes
held court
Deals were made
Times were good
How green was the Valley
that flowed with
milk and honey?
It was Paradise ....

© 1997 Evelyn Rhodes

Doyle and Davis were among the first black Car Dealers in the country

Courtesy of Richard Thomas Collection

Courtesy of Richard Thomas Collection

I Got It

Just plain old black asphalt in
America.
White bonnet, broad brimmed
Ribbons the color of royalty
Push cart dressed all up
Rainbow sheets
Big sign red and white
I got it....

City street Gypsy selling his
wares
Skillets, pots, an almost-cashmere
sweater
Crooked label from Saks
Bent bicycle wheel shining like a
new dime

A real pearl necklace, zircon
diamond rings
From the Five and Ten six rolls of
Louie XIV wallpaper
Two bottles — Nature Boy,

Cadillac Club
One half-empty one half-full
Out of the sides of his mouth.

If I ain't got it today
I'll have it tomorrow
Tell me what you need
I got it.

Whatever Happened

Whatever happened to the time
when everything
was black and white without the
shade of gray?
When it didn't seem like life was
so chaotic;
When you were lost, you could
find your way.
When the sky was blue and the
grass was green
In the day — you worked, at
night — you dreamed.

Whatever happened to the time
when there was only right and
wrong?
When people loved each other
for what they were and everyone
belonged
Was there such a time?
Or was it just a fantasy
Conjured deep inside of me.
A dream of equality for everyone
To be passed on from father to
son.

Yes whatever happened to the
time
When everything was black and
white
without the shade of gray?
Like the morning dew exposed
to the rays of the sun;
It slowly melted away....

Straight Talk

I am Detroit
a strait city
wet and mild

I am Detroit
arsenal of Democracy
midwestern melting pot over-
flowing it banks
with multilingual sounds and
voices

I am Detroit
motor city
motor town
Motown
of music and mechanical fame

Bring me your tired and
your poor for $5 a day

I am Detroit
the brown bomber
fist in your face
the X place
from which Detroit Red came

I am Detroit
I am music
Smokey & Stevie & Marvin &
Temptations
Aretha & Sir Roland & John Lee...
the beat keeps going on & on
like the sound on the line
the beat keeps going on & on
like the sound on the line.

PARADISE
VALLEY

Carlton Plaza Hotel *Burton Historical Library*

John White — Owner of Gotham Hotel
Courtesy Richard Thomas Collection

BILTMORE HOTEL

CARVER HOTEL

WELCOME TO THE GOTHAM — It's written all over the place — welcome to clean, comfortable, restful rooms. Private bath, radio, telephone and television in all rooms *Courtesy Richard Thomas Collection*

The Great Black Strip

Before the freeways were built, even before the riot of 43, there was a strip in Detroit called Paradise Valley, and it was swinging all night long...

By TONI JONES
Free Press Staff Writer

Count Basie's band wailed "After Hours" thinly from the juke box, but the small gathering in the Garfield Lounge of the Randora Hotel hardly heard. The faces and clothes were 1972, different. Drinks were more expensive. And the music didn't croon live and bittersweet as it did 30 years ago. Gone were the handsome, smooth talking sporting men dressed in Al Capone suits with money in their pockets and beautiful women on their sleeves. Gone too were the big bands, the long shiny chauffeur-driven limousines, the high-ceilinged dance halls with their crystal chandeliers and the chorus girls in puffed sleeved satin dresses with low cut backs, floppy brimmed hats and cigarette holders.

The Randora Lounge at 98 Garfield now comprises almost all that's left to suggest the frenzied night life and the people who made this part of Black Bottom distinctly and uniquely Paradise Valley. The valley burgeoned in the early 30's along and around Adams and St. Antione shortly before, after — and some because of — the legalization of whiskey in 1933. It included nearly all the black businesses in the densely populated black section of Detroit. It was centered in Black Bottom the name given the area which housed most of the city's blacks whose boundaries extended from Hastings to Brush and from Gratiot to Vernor Highway.

The business district containing black owned shops, music stores, grocery stores, bowling alleys, hotels, bars and lucrative policy offices, was all called Paradise Valley. The Valley was open 24 hours a day as were its restaurants, gambling houses and the after hour clubs where the best whiskey in town, legal and illegal flowed steadily for 25 cents an ounce.

The Valley attracted all of the best black entertainers in the country. And many aspiring young singers, dancers and musicians got their first big break before the audience at the Club Plantation and the 666. Earl Hines, The Inkspots, the Will Mastin Trio, Billie Holiday, Duke Ellington, Cab Calloway and Dinah Washington were Valley regulars. They were booked into the Greystone Ballroom or the Michigan Theater or any of a dozen other big white-only nightclubs or gathering places, but they were only welcome there during show time.

Racial discrimination, especially in the downtown hotels, forced black performers to stay in black hotels when they were in the Valley. Hotels included the *Dewey*, the *Biltmore* and the *Norwood*, which was best known for its shows staged on a revolving floor in the Hotel's Club Plantation. Ella Fitzgerald, Billy Eckstine, Sugar Brown, and the McKinney's Cotton Pickers were frequent performers.

Dance groups featuring long-legged beauties like Mitzi, Mary and Mike (the 3M's) or Ziggy Johnson's dance productions were familiar shows at the Chocolate Bar, the Plantation and Club 666. Tap dancers Baby Lawrence, Durb Wilson and some of the best performers in town unabashedly practiced their show routines on the sidewalk in front of the Carlton hotel. Crime was practically nonexistent.

Valley regulars included Uncle Dan, who lent whiskey money to his friends and always had a spare $1,000. Uncle Dan would sit outside the Turf bar or Lee Lucky's to

606 Horse Shoe Bar and Other Businesses
Burton Historical Library

shoot the breeze with passersby and he was never robbed. Black policemen assigned to patrol the Valley partied with the night crowd, but they set absolute rules forbidding criminal disorder.

Characters like Buffalo James, owner of a prosperous restaurant was often seen socializing with the cooks and entertainers when the restaurant was empty. As the ballroom closed and the hungry night-clubers began looking for a place to eat, Buffalo would stand outside the restaurant with a big white handkerchief in his hand. When he spotted groups of people coming toward the restaurant, he would signal the cooks to start stirring and the band to start playing by wiping his face with a large white cloth. Another favorite figure was Sonny Bronson, a temperamental bartender who owned a sandwich shop but refused to serve anyone who yelled at him or made him angry.

Courtesy of Richard Thomas Collection

"It used to look like a carnival on the weekends," recalled Jimmy (The Greek) Johnson, who owned a couple of pool halls in the Valley. "You could go from club to club and after three in the morning, you'd have the thrill of listening to a jam session.

"Say for instance, Earl Hines' band was playing somewhere in Flint, Basie's band in Pontiac and Duke's band would be over here at the Greystone and maybe Cab's band would be playing somewhere else in the state. They would all stay here (in the Valley) and go to the places by bus and come back here at night. When they came back, all these musicians would get together and stay up and jam all night, playing all of their songs. Sometimes, they would jam until 10 or 11 a.m. the next morning," he said.

The heart of the Valley's economy was the *Policy* operation, later replaced by the *Numbers*. It was generally believed and accepted that the only way a black man could make a lot of money was to run a policy house. Unlike the numbers, policy houses — which were exclusively black-owned and operated — had a reputation for honesty. The policy was played by buying three numbers for five cents. The numbers ranged from one to 78. Twelve winning numbers were drawn daily and paid odds of 500-1 or $25 for a nickel.

Gradually policy houses gave way to the numbers operation. It was a common sight for those allowed near the money to see $150,000 in cash in a safe with the door wide open. The next day, however the same safe might be wiped clean from one day's winning pay offs.

"It (the numbers) was a game of the percentages and they managed to make money out of it," said one of the Valley's ex-patrons. "But it was based on the daily races and you could pick up a newspaper — because they published the race results — and anybody who knew how could figure the number. When the numbers came out that's what it was. Even kids knew how to pick the numbers out of the paper.

"But there was still gambling all over the place. One man had a club upstairs over the Turf Bar and it was open 24 hours a day. "They played poker and black jack. One of the things they always had a hard time selling the police on in this city was crap shooting. Police didn't allow any crap shooting in the Valley.

"At that time you had all of the politicians, council members, the mayor and big people in the police department who use to come down there," he said.

Many skilled black comptometer operators, adding machine operators, secretaries, stenographers, accountants and lawyers served their apprenticeships in policy and number houses in the Valley. Before the policy operations, few black owned businesses required highly trained help. But policy money came in so fast that adding machine workers soon became proficient and well paid.

In August, 1939, the policy opera-tion received a severe blow. A policy house bookkeeper, Mrs. Janet McDonald, murdered her child, and committed suicide when her boyfriend, who allegedly was connected with protection payoffs to police officials, ended their affair. Letters she had written and addressed to local newspapers, the governor, and the Federal Bureau of Investigation charged that her former boyfriend was the collection agent of illegal money for the police department. The papers were near her body.

Circuit Court Judge Homer Ferguson was appointed to conduct an inquiry. A special prosecutor, Chester O'Hara, was appointed to handle the investigation when the prosecutor, Duncan McCrea, was disqualified by charges of his involvement in the conspiracy to protect gamblers. A mayoral aide, who testified that he collected money from racketeers for the mayor, said he delivered more than $3,000 from policy operators to Mayor Richard Reading in his City Hall office.

The prosecutor's key witness also testified that one of the convicted racketeers had told him of a plan to set up a special racket squad in 1938 to help the numbers operators. Other witnesses charged that Reading had accepted $55,000 in payments to "protect" the $10-million-a-year Detroit operation.

By June, 1942, Reading, his son Richard Reading Jr., the mayor's administrative assistant, McCrea, several policy operators, including Joe Louis' manager, the former sheriff, the police superintendent, and 20 police officers were convicted of graft conspiracy. But the scandal only enhanced the glamour of the Valley.

Joe Louis, the Valley's beloved "Brown Bomber," was still in his prime and Sugar Ray Robinson was a promising young boxer. Each time the Bomber fought, mobs of Louis fans huddled into stores, shops or restaurants with radios to hear him slug out another victory. Whites in Chauffeur-driven cars would ride through the Valley after victories carrying black riders on top of the cars. Everyone shared the booze and good feelings. When Louis wasn't training or managing his Chicken Shack on the outskirts of the Valley, or running from Broadway Joe (one of Louis' friends who would catch a taxi to chase the boxer about ten blocks to ask for a few dollars), Louis was partying in the Valley.

T-Bone steaks at The Hole cost 35 cents. A bologna sandwich on toast at Biddy's Restaurant was a nickel. "Duke Ellington's band would always stop by Biddy's for a nickel sandwich when they were in town," said Jesse Faithful, owner of Valley Foods Restaurant, 1719 St. Antione, one of the last remaining shops of Paradise Valley. "I don't know how I ever made a sandwich for a nickel. This place is empty now, but at one time I had eight waitresses and four cooks. The expressway (Chrysler) took that away.

"This whole street used to be some kind of night club or bar. If you came to Detroit from another town and the cab driver asked where you wanted to go, every black person would say Paradise Valley," Faithful said, looking through the front window of his restaurant which now seats only 15 customers and sells bologna sandwiches for 40 cents.

"There was gambling in about every other joint, usually upstairs. My building was adjoining one of the biggest number houses in the area. It was originally suppose to be a bank, but it didn't work out too well, so it was turned into a numbers house and eventually became a real estate office.

"The Norwood was torn down about seven years ago. The Biltmore was just up the street where the Stroh's parking lot is now. They bought the Norwood and sold it to Hudson's for the warehouse. "They've (Stroh's) been here nine times trying to buy this property but I'm not going to sell for anything less than $75,000. This is valuable property and a lot of rich Negroes who owned property down here sold for almost nothing."

Dunbar Hospital —Detroit's First Black Hospital was named for the poet Paul Laurence Dunbar— Burton Historical Library

Burton Historical Library

Every two years by popular vote the Valley elected a mayor who promised fried chicken in every skillet and pork chops in every ice box and claimed to have direct contact with City Hall. The title Mayor was also given to leaders of Bronzeville in Chicago and Cleveland, Sepia City in Toledo, and Harlem in New York. Roy Lightfoot, one the Valley's first mayors and owner of B&C Club and Long's Drug Store, used his drug store as a central information center. If someone died, disappeared or was in the hospital, relatives and friends could call Long's for the latest information.

While much of the sporting life continued to flourish in the Valley during the early 40's, new businesses began to open on John R near Canfield. Black servicemen who ate their last breakfast at the Norwood Hotel before being shipped overseas during World War II returned to find that the Valley had been replaced by a Las Vegas-like strip along John R.

Instead of meeting at El Sino's, Peking or Cookie's Restaurant, the social hour and the chi-chi place to be seen shifted to the Ebony room of the Gotham Hotel or the Wal Ha Lounge of the Garfield Hotel. "Cookie's Place was quite prominent at one time," said James Cookie, the former owner who works part-time now as a bellman at the St. Regis Hotel. "My clientele was mixed. During that time, whites weren't afraid to go to black clubs. Integration had just started and Negro entertainers began to move out to other hotels. Soon anybody who was anyone would stay in the white hotels. People left the Gotham, which was a fine hotel, to go downtown to the Sheraton and Hilton.

"We had been in business for 26 years. Our place was open 24-hours and we would gross $1,000 every night. We were never held up once in all those years," Cookie said. "When we left in 1963, we were just about the last ones to go. Now I hate to go over there because it brings back memories."

Mounting racial tensions were largely ignored until June 20, 1943, when two black youths were arrested for starting a fight with white youths on the Belle Isle Bridge. The black youths later claimed that they were seeking revenge after being ejected from Eastwood Park by white youths a few days earlier. Before police could quell the argument, a 17-year-old black spread the rumor that a black woman and her baby had been thrown off the Belle Isle Bridge by whites and both had drowned. More than 200 enraged blacks and whites began a wild fighting spree.

Police used tear gas to clear the bridge but small fights broke out along E. Jefferson. Later that night, rumors spread to the Forest Club recreation center on East Forest. A checkroom operator at the club announced the report over a microphone in the dance hall. Rioting spread along Hastings, St. Antione, Brush and John R from east grand Boulevard to the river. White mobs attacked a group of blacks in the Roxy Theater on Woodward then went after black pedestrians.

The riot was ended the next day when 4,000 army troops were sent under martial law into the city. Although troops never fired a shot, 35 people were killed, 530 injured and 1,300 arrested. Many of the blacks who lived in Black Bottom began to flee for fear that another riot would eventually repeat itself in their neighborhood. The new homeowners began buying houses in white neighborhoods surrounding 12th street.

After the riots, the Gotham Hotel, a previously white-owned 300 room-luxury hotel at 111 Orchestra Place, was sold for $200,000 to a black group reputedly connected with the numbers operation. Like the Valley in its prime, "The Strip" was mobbed with night-clubers waiting outside the Garfield Lounge, Sonnie Wilson's, the Chesterfield Lounge, The Flame, and the Forest Club to catch the late floor shows. But some of the friendliness was gone.

Entertainers such as Josephine Baker, Lionel Hampton, Sarah Vaughn and Nat (King) Cole were as familiar to the strips as they were to other tourist spots in the country. By the late 1950's, the strip began to fade as more black people started buying homes near the 12th Street area. And by 1962, the Gotham had closed after a series of raids destroyed the hotel which allegedly served as the clearing house for Detroit's $12-million numbers racket. In March 1963, the Garfield Hotel burned. Guest and residents leaped from second floor windows after the flames that started in the kitchen blocked their escape down the front and rear stairs. Two residents were killed, and the Garfield, once a focal point of Paradise Valley, was destroyed.

Urban League —Played a prominent role in Black Society. It was also the place where the Elite held Debutant Balls for their daughters. Some of the old-timers say, however, that to be a member of that crowd, the girls had to be of the *High Yellow* variety or her parents had to have lots of money. Don't know for sure, but probably true.

The Randora Hotel which was being built as an annex to the Garfield by Randolph Wallace, owner of the Garfield Hotel, was completed but the guest list changed. When Wallace died a few months later, plans to convert the once lively strip into a medical center were finalized. Some of the people who frequent the Garfield Lounge in the Randora still remember the old days. Paradise Valley, The Strip. The sophisticated set and the night crowds have been replaced by thugs, junkies and winos.

Integration and prosperity have forced the city to expand its boundaries to the edges of newly developed suburbs. Slowly, night life and entertainment — with the perfection of modern stereophonic equipment — have become home affairs. Night-clubers are more sedate now and reluctant to travel outside their own neighborhoods. What was once a swinging town — a place where free spirits and sporting folks from New York, Chicago, Cleveland and nearby states could come together on the weekends — is only a memory.

Article reprinted with permission of the Detroit Free Press. Article dated January 7, 1973

Mr. & Mrs Charles C. Diggs —*Colored Detroit - Burton Historical Library*

— Eleanor Roosevelt (Center) at Brewster Project Ground-breaking —
Courtesy of The Orlin Jones Collection

Our Folks

Each and every passing day,
Our folks gave us what we need,
Neighbors, friends and relatives,
They all gave us what we need,
They gave us pride and dignity,
They gave us faith in our ability,
They gave us strength to bear the
trials,
They gave us wisdom when just
a child,
The Golden Rule,
The importance of school,
The love to carry us through,
The knowledge and truth to
understand,
No matter how cruel the pain,
And when we're alone,
These things keep us strong,
Cause folks gave us what we
need....

© *1997 Marie A. Berry*

The Garden

Turn the earth
from the top
of Black Bottom
and bring back
memories of a place
within a place

Use ebony hands
to sift through
grains of shifting
ebony magical shapes
these challenged those
unlawful forces unafraid
to grow Paradise from urban
blight
and echo unrestrained freedom.

Emerge Paradise Valley
from old-African-identities
Spring forth
Up past
restrictive injustice
to backhand racism
in the face
using cultural imagination
and comely grace

Dark-merging-bottom-
types
combine to shove, push
aside urban poverty
and reveal unlimited
possibilities
from sweat engendering
Character
A human community
whose sense of
responsibility
baptized dark bottom
earth

Re-emerge repositors
of enduring values,
their wisdom inspired,
nurturing the dark
imaged roots
which reach deep down
into Black Bottom earth
Turning it over from the
top....

© *1997 Cheryl Wells*

Family

The family is life and like light
Trolleys down many bizarre and
challenging roads.
But like a sanctuary,
is pregnant with odors
And colors where virtues are
bestowed.
And love, peace, and promise
dwell therein,
And on the checkered
calendar of time
Generations unfold.
The family is like a magnificent
tapestry,
A tapestry of the soul
layered with intricate
stitches of love
and memories more precious
than gold.

© *1997 James Neal Ware*

L. to R. Beatrice Buck, Marion Buck Gregory, Marie Champion, Blanche Champion, Christine Buck
Courtesy of Beatrice Buck Collection

Paradise
(In the Valley)

Paradise
is embodied in the myriad
images
of our wistful dreams
and lofty desires;

Paradise
lives
in our hope
for boundless happiness
and freedom eternal

© 1997 Heather Buchanan

MISS MABEL WHITING
Executive Secretary, St. Aubin Branch, Y. W. C. A.

Dr. Pharr C. Freeman, MD - *Courtesy of the Hilda Vest Collection*

Submitted by Peggy A. Moore

Peggy A. Moore, Age 12

Love Child

Small hands caress
mine
With love and devotion
Holding on for dear life
With enough slack left
For needed separation
Important departure
I'll try not to hold on
Too tight
For too long....

© 1997 Teresa Tucker Moore

DETROIT CONTENDER

Black Bottom Boys — *Submitted by Elvenia McCowin*

Robert Williams *Submitted by Geraldine Metoyer*

Little Bill Lawrence —*Submitted by Peggy A. Moore*

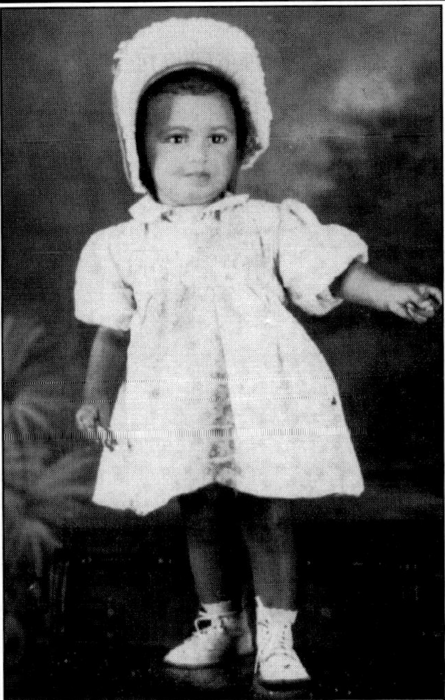

Rose Emma Franklin - *Submitted by Geraldine Metoyer*

Jucy

Heaven's little gift
that never arrived.
Velvet coffee skin,
chocolate, tootsie roll eyes.
Big round cheeks,
soft and sweet like cotton candy.
Flashing a toothless grin
that says all is fine and dandy.

I longed to read you
stories at night,
while tucked so cozy in bed.
Oh, why you never came
I just don't know.
Was it something I did or said?

Visions of washing little hands
and kissing little toes
still come to me late at night.
Dreams of your voice saying
"Mommy" so sweet,
gives my heart pure delight!

I don't question why
the world is round,
or how clouds can hold
so much rain.
I don't question Einstein's
Theory,
Beethoven's gift,
or why you never came.

© 1997 Evelyn Phosia Holmes

Simple Pleasures

Oh, how simple
were the pleasures
I remember as a child,
Gazing upward to the heavens,
Making figures of the clouds.
Nestled in the warmth
of sunshine

Through tightly-closed eyelids
I could see
Golden sparkles of
bright light rays
Dancing 'round me playfully.
And the petals of the daisy,
One by one, would cast their lot
To be the last one to remain

Balanced the passion
of my heart.
Oh, how simple
were the pleasures
I remember as a child,

Enchanted by life's
countless wonders
Trusting her woes
would be reconciled.
How my soul yearns
to be shaken
And my sleepy heart awakened
To the joy of simple pleasures
Once again.

© 1996 Dianne A. Rhodes

Spirit to Achieve

To see the beauty
in this life,
To walk with
open hearts,
Not thirsty for a soul to hate,
Or trying to find a fault,
But seeing
every person,
Every child,
as human beings,
With hopes and dreams,
And by all means,
The spirit
to achieve....

© 1997 Marie A. Berry

Roxie Smith, Dorothy Robinson, & Pauline Moore
Submitted by Peggy A. Moore

St. Peter Clavery Nursery School — The place where working mothers left their children (1948)

Submitted by Peggy A. Moore

Submitted by Robert J. Haynes

Courtesy of Jacqueline Caffey Collection

Paradise Valley & Black Bottom School Children

Submitted by Jeanette Vaughn

A 3 Feet Wonder Of The World

(Dedicated to D'wan Sims and all the other missing children)

D'wan Sims
D. 0. B. 10-29-90
3' tall/50 lbs
Missing 12-11-94

I wonder as he wanders
From a land of wonder
From 3 feet, the world
looks so strange
50 lbs is such a small
weight to carry
But the weight of his loss
Is so great and growing
Add to all the other missings

These are political acts
Like the disappearings
In many foreign countries
Tear drops
Continuing tear drops
A chain of tears
Connecting all our pain
For the losses
Of children who are
and could be
Brothers, sisters, husbands,
wives, and fathers

Wonder as I wander
Where is D'wan this
Day, this night, this minute
As all those days
I forgot about him and
Those living only on
Milk cartons and in
The hearts of their families.

© *1997 ejlli Williams*

Rap On

A Lesson in Black History

Some historians have said that rapping may have begun with Africans sitting together telling their fellow tribesmen stories of all kinds.

When Blacks were enslaved
many years ago
There were many things
they weren't allowed to know.
They weren't allowed to read
or even own a book.
The only things they could do
was farm, clean, and cook.

But slaves really wanted
to read and to write,
So they peeked at books,
but only in the night.
Soon the slaves were freed
and did many good things.
Writing books, singing songs,
and inventing things.

Carter G. Woodson once said,
"Understand
That history includes
our fellow Black man."
He's the Father of Black History,
so to speak.
He's the man who started
Negro History Week.

George Washington Carver
who was never a bore
Is the man who planted peanuts
and a whole lot more.
He made so many things
from one little plant,
Shoe polish and some soap.
Yeh, how about that.

Harriet Tubman, Oh Yeh,
you've heard the name,
She's the lady on the freedom
railroad train.
But she didn't really ride
a fast train you know;
It was a path to freedom
where some slaves could go.

And it was Charles Richard Drew
whom we should thank.
He was the man who
started the first blood bank.
We celebrate the life
of Martin Luther King
Who said peaceful marches
will "Let Freedom Ring."

But remember fellow students
don't get us wrong;
We can't put all Black History
in one little song.
If there's any more
that you'd like to know,
To your local library,
you must go.

Get a book — and read.
Oh, come on — just read.
It won't hurt — to read.

© *1998 Barbara Pattee*

This Generation

This generation,
like all generations, declare
They have arrived,
Unlike the last, unlike the past,
In fact, we will survive.

Our days and nights
are not like yours,
You did not live and breath$_e$
You did not see the rising sun,
You did not love like me...

This generation,
this new generation, declare
"We're brave and bold,"
while imitating days gone by,
Until they, too... grow old.

© *1997 Marie A. Berry*

The Coetts — Founded by Mary Agnes Davis in 1941. It served as a Civic & Social Organization for young ladies. *Courtesy of the Hilda Vest Collection*

For My Son

For you, my son
I'll do what I can
To teach you the values
That will make you a man
I'll know you'll be safe
With decisions everyday
I hope my love and guidance
Will lead you the right way
I can only show you the path
In life that you should take
The journey, you alone
Will have to make
I can't teach you wisdom
That will come in time
Listen to your heart
And follow your own mind
All I can do
Is the best that I can
And with help from the Lord
My son, you will
Be a man....

© 1997 Rita Diane Hudgens

Yellow Bus

Yellow bus, yellow bus
why are you so slow?
I wish you'd come back,
I'm ready to go.

I wish I knew,
said the little girl in blue.
I'm waiting for the yellow bus
to take me home, too.

Where did it go?
asked the little boy in red.
If it doesn't come back,
we'll have to walk instead.

Well, I'm not moving,
said the little boy in black.
I'm not moving
till the bus comes back.

So they waited and they waited
under the yellow bus sign,
neatly in a row,
all standing in line.

Their minds filled with ideas
of why the bus was late.
But the only thing they could do
was be patient and just wait.

Soon they heard a sound
that roared like thunder,
their little eyes were bright
with surprise and wonder.

For soon their fears
were a thing of the past,
when the yellow bus came
to take them home at last.

© 1997 Latres Orr

The Seed

He planted the seed
then he wanted to go
I was left to nurture it
and watch it grow
I cultivated it with love
took care of its needs
Tried to keep away
all the ugly weeds
In the warmth of love
as it started to grow
I spoke about the things
it would need to know
I watered it daily with patience,
understanding and praise
Giving it strength against the
wind
on cold, dark days
Now, stands before me
a strong, sturdy tree
Bearing the fruits of knowledge
and integrity
And I take pride
in what I've done
You were his seed
but you are
My son....

© 1997 Rita Diane Hudgens

My Grandmother

My grandmother,
my dearest friend
One of my favorite people
right to the end
She always wanted me —to be
the best that I could be
And whenever I fell,
she would help me to my feet
My grandmother,
sometimes, got very mad
Then she'd stop and say,
"I guess things ain't so bad."
The treasures and the gifts
she possessed
When she was alive,
Oh how I was blessed.
My grandmother, I miss her
so much these days,
But it was her time,
so the Lord took her away
Still, I know she is with me,
by my side in the spirit
And all that she taught me,
Lord knows, I still hear it
My grandmother had such
a wonderful smile
Warm like the coat she bought,
when I was a child
She was always there
when I needed her
Cared for all the kids,
no matter whose they were
My grandmother truly
walked with Grace
Homecooking, no one could
match her taste
All those sweet rolls, cakes, and
steaming hot pies
Cooking for us a delight, you
could see in her eyes
My grandmother, all the things in
life we shared
I know she loved us,
I know she cared
The day it all went down,
and her life came to an end
I told her, "Grandmother, I will
miss you, but we will...
meet again."

© 1997 Teresa M. Brown

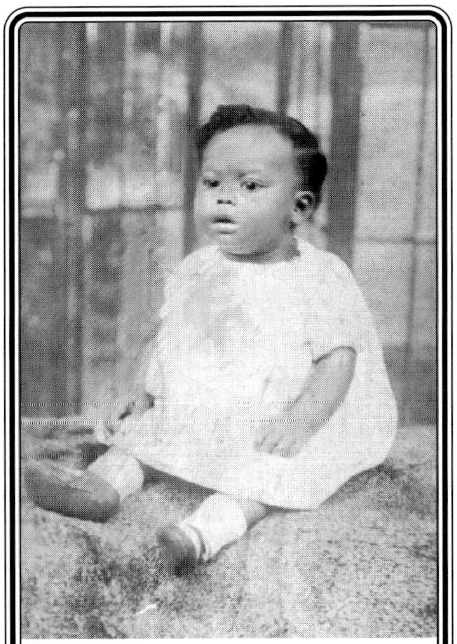

Jewel Martin's Baby Picture - *Courtesy of Jewel Martin*

Charles Davis - *Courtesy of Jewel Martin*

Butterflies and Puppy Chases

The innocence
in children's eyes
a puppy chasing butterflies
it does not linger long,
or still nor does
the puppy think it will.
As innocence erodes with time
its lessons painted on our faces
maturation spoils the fun
of butterflies and puppy chases.

© 1991 Sharon Smith-Knight
Selection from "Wine Sip" Broadside Press

The Detroit Urban League — The League was founded in 1916 to look after the social needs of the Negroes. Its primary focus was Health, Employment, Recreation, and Housing. Its Community Center was located at 1564 Chestnut Street. One half of The Board of Directors was white and the other half colored.

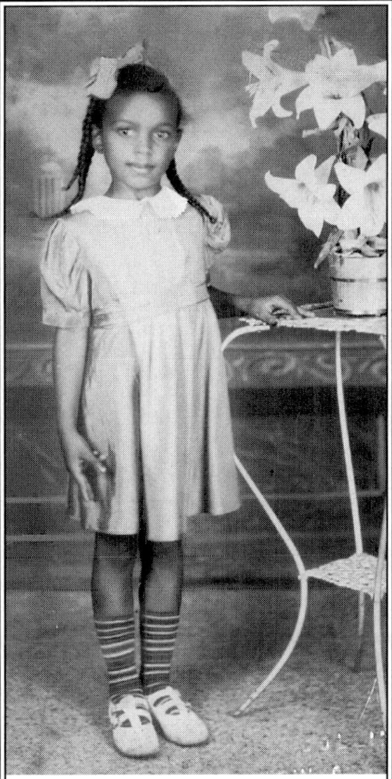

Geraldine Williams 1940 — *submitted by Geraldine Metoyer*

Eternal Love

I wake up every morning,
Looking for the sun;
Living a life of iniquity,
Having carnal fun:

I travel with my so-called friends,
Whom I would never duck;
And a haughty individual,
Whom I call Lady Luck:

She's really quite a person,
A victor of her bout;
But I awaken one evening
and found
My luck had just ran out.

Then Jesus came into my life,
And washed away my sins.
He turned my darkness into light,
And allowed the Comforter in.

He placed angels all around me,
I thought for my protection;
But they nurture me slowly
everyday
Towards spiritual perfection.

Smiling, happy angels,
as far as I can see,
They're looking down on
the House of God,
They're blessing you,
They're blessing me.

And far above the horizon,
Sitting on their throne;
God and Jesus are telling us,
We'll never be alone.

God bellowed across
the universe,
Whatever you must do;
Remember the power
of my word,
I'm not through blessing you.

And up from the doldrums
rising high,
To heights far above;
We're being blessed with
a heavenly gift,
The gift of Eternal Love.

© 1997 Deacon Marble Brown
Selection from "Rhymes of Our Times"
Galactic Publishing Company

St. James Baptist Church — *Courtesy of Richard Thomas Collection*

Second Baptist Church— Played a Major Role in the Underground Railroad during times of slavery — *Submitted by Herbert Metoyer*

Home

Ten days after I willfully
surrendered my life to Christ,
the Comforter came
and now lives in me.
I have gently become
transformed and reshaped,
Spiritually aroused of my senses.
His voice is seldom heard
but more felt within
my inner being,
the essence of who I really am.
Now, I am of His Flock
Learning daily to recognize
His Voice and Presence
within me.
And when He moves,
like an expectant mother,
I feel His Character all around me
and my flesh tingles with chills.
Furthermore, as I read His *Word*,
I become engrossed
as in a novel.
For I am indulged, motivated,
marveled, encouraged,
I have become... well, stimulated.
I am learning to meditate
His *Wisdom* into my life,
understanding, of course,
that His *Foresight* is for my
"Return Home," not my
destruction.
Therefore, I have accepted
His *Help* for this journey
I must take,
as I prepare to fulfill
that of me which longs to be
reacquainted with "Home"
again!

© 1994 Andre Terry

Is There A Heaven For a G.

You speak of a place
I've never heard
And of a white-boy
who heals with His every word
But all that means little to me
Cause I don't think there's
a heaven for a G.
I've lived a life
of thuggery and fame
Terror filled the mind
at the mention of my name
But I can't change the things
I was or will be,
Does that mean
He'll still open up
His Kingdom for me?
If what you say is true,
then I'm sure I won't last,
And I'll die like I lived,
young and fast.
But one day, for myself,
I'm sure I'll see
If there really is
a Heaven for a G.

© 1996 V. duwon Jackson

After The Storm

I am like a rainbow
that glides across
the sky of time
remains awhile — a-shine
in the element that
abides by the Law of Grace

I cannot change
nor alter my place
in the sky
mounted like a jewel
a precious outlined
frame of light

But then,
I am not my own
in this perfect sky
that captures all the beauty
my iridescent hue.

After the storm and rain
look up
I will be there

© 1985 Dwjuana Terrell

DETROIT PEOPLES NEWS

Faith

Faith can move mountains.
Trust in the Lord
Like children trusting their father
To provide food, shelter and
clothing.
Even when you are old and gray
Trust His ageless wisdom
Know that He watches over you
Day and night.
Hold onto His hand,
Trust Him all you can.
He will make everything all right.
In happy times, sad times,
Lonely times,
Grief and sorrow times,
You can still have joy,
If you have the faith
That can move mountains!

© 1997 Caroline Adams

On this day...

On this day...
I vow to fast
as well as pray...
that God guide
our husbands, our sons,
our uncles, our leaders,
our fathers, our teachers,
our nephews, our brothers
through...
their rites/rights of passage
and the world
read clearly
the Black Man's Message.
On this day I pray!

© 1997 Rain Africa Reign

Central United Methodist Church — Submitted by Herbert Metoyer

and filled with the Holy Ghost.

The word of God has filled me,
with victory, joy, and pep,
and my spirit's overflowing
even though I've slowed my steps.
As you are today, I was yesterday;
And in closing, I add with sorrow,
as I am today,
You will surely be tomorrow!
I AM A SENIOR!!

© 1997 Deacon Marble Brown
Selection from "Rhymes of Our Times"
Galactic Publishing Company

I Am A Senior

I am a senior, I was born
a little before your time,
And the things we did as children,
would probably blow your mind:
We had places to go, things to do,
and games we would play;
Games that you've heard of,
but wouldn't play today.
We shot marbles,
we pitched horseshoes;
we played tag ball,
and kick the cans;
Spin the bottle, Hide and seek,
and shot spit-balls
with rubber bands;
We built model planes,
and built kites that flew
as high as you could see,
and I really got upset,
when mine
got caught up in a tree.

Old tin cans and bottles,
we shot with BB guns;
We made our bows and arrows,
and push carts, all by hand.
Sling shots cut from inner tubes,
that we used for rubber bands.
We rode sleighs all winter;
summer we rode bikes,
And on holidays
we'd go to 'Belle Island,
to simply take a hike.
My mother didn't call
the gas company
when our house got cold;
We used gas for cooking and
cleaning,
we heated our house with coal.
Refrigerators were for the wealthy,
we had no TV's or games that rock
No VCR's made by Magnavox;
and our food sometimes spoiled
in our old ice box.

But on Saturdays,
we would celebrate,
or so the story goes;
All the neighborhood children,
could be found in the neighbor-
hood shows.
On Sundays, we went to church,
morning, noon and night;
And my Mother often asked me;
"What did you learn from the
Book of Life?"
I grew up and went astray,
and lived a life of sin;
And never really came alive,
'Til I let Jesus in.
Today I stand before you,
beside your gracious host,
Saved, sanctified, baptized,

Jesus Is A Friend of Mine

(*Name Dropper*)

Whenever I stumble down
He picks me up off the ground.
He's my Savior,
A good Man to have around.

When I need Him in a special case,
He'll come right here
to this very place.
He's so real to me,
I can almost touch His face.

Jesus is a friend of mine,
We're together all the time.
Do you know Him?
Well, He's a friend of mine....

When I look and see
the rising sun,
I praise His name for all the great
things He has done.
He's my Savior,
And me— I'm the lucky one.

I know some folks just don't
understand,
Why I put my life within His hand.
Well, He's my Savior,
And YES — I love the Man...

© 1979 Herbert R. Metoyer

I Know That He's Still There

Another year has come and gone,
and we have a lot to share.
Another era has come to life,
and no-one seems to care.
Another dream has been fulfilled,
one less burden to bear.
I'll send praises up to my God,
I know that He's still there!

Another grave has been dug,
a child is laid to rest.
Another Saint is put out front,
to pass a crucial test.
I'm glad to know
that the God I serve,
knows what I can bear.
I'll send up praises to my God,
I know that He's still there!

Another babe has been born,
to live a righteous life,
Another hand reaching to God,
to rid itself of strife;
Another soul to learn of the Love,
that Jesus has to share,
I'll send up praises to my God,
I know that He's still there!

Forget the troubles of the world
and the things you can't bear.
Forget our trials and valleys
that we must often share.
Remember God, His word,
and His tender-loving care.
And send praises up to our God,
and know that He's still there!

© 1997 Deacon Marble Brown
Selection from "Rhymes of Our Times"
Galactic Publishing Company

***St. Mathew Episcopal Church** — Submitted by Herbert Metoyer*

St. Matthews Episcopal Church

First founded in 1847. But because of the Fugitive Slave Law, many of its members fled to Canada and other places where their safety and freedom were assured. The church then was dormant until 1880. Under the leadership of Rev. Dr. George Washington followed by Rev G. Mott Williams, the last site at St. Antoine and Elizabeth Street was purchased and a building erected in 1884....

YWCA One of the best places to eat in town —*Submitted By Herbert Metoyer*

DETROIT PEOPLES NEWS

Ladies of Josephat

They walked the mortared
brick of St. Antoine,
high-top shoes laced all the way
up,
Onto Beaubien where the street
car ran.
Beaded and cross-chained,
they lock-stepped from the sand,
red-walled-chapel of St. Josephat,
past the three copper-colored
iron balls of the pawn shop,
down to our block,
across Brush to Canfield.
It was whispered around
that they were witches and
gypsies
from the old country.
I didn't know any better.
Struck dumb, I just watched
them.
Celled in brown and white
habits,
their dark vanilla faces
smuggled out smiles,
as they walked past us.
From the gait of their steps,
I thought I heard an old spiritual
chant
first remembered in a sanctified
storefront church on Forest
Street.

Yes, I beat the Devil running
And I'm on my way to Heaven
And the world can do me no harm

© 1991 Murray Jackson
Selection from "Watermelon Seeds & Cherry Pits," Broadside Press

Twin Flames

Divine love, true love
Created before time begun
God's Glory — a Holy Love Story
Twin souls and
God reigning as one.
Hypnotic has been
God's breath of life
Through the ages, we have
listened to him speak
Divinely guided
by his everlasting love
Our world without end shall
never be weak
Transformed by the power
of our love
Even dark waters
turn crystal clean
One light, one soul,
so strong, so true
No form of evil dares
to venture near
You touch my stomach
and I am filled
I open my eyes
so that you may see
Manly presence standing in
female essence
Endlessly united in
perpetual majesty.

Twin flames, love's desire
in eternal fire
God's will on earth be done
Reborn this day,
so that we may live
Our flame more brilliant
than the sun....

© 1998 Dr. Barbara Ann Woodson

Gathering

Me and my little brother "Babes"
are thoroughly baptized
in the bathtub by Mom
Saturday night.

Sunday morning, Second Baptist
Church, Monroe Street
We ride the Beaubien streetcar
all the way downtown.
The conductor with his
stingy-brim cap
flips the seats North
for the trip back.

I grumble to Sunday School
and sometimes church
to hear Reverend Bradley
preach about the Spirit
and Frederick Douglass who
came to talk here once.

The Amens are done,
we are on our way
back to Canfield, fried chicken,
crisp brown and hot,
white rice piled high next to
steaming collard greens.
Hot biscuits thirsting for marga-
rine colored the night before.

Then waste the rest of the day
scraping, washing dumb ol'
dishes, pots and pans.

© 1991 Murray Jackson
Selection from "Watermelon Seeds & Cherry Pits," Broadside Press

When Mom Paid Tax Streetcar Trip Was Daughter's Fun

by
Dorothy Kimble

The old City Hall Building was torn down quite a few years ago, but the old County Building still is standing in downtown Detroit on Randolph Street.

View of Woodward Avenue 1952 — *Burton Historical Library*

My mother, Pearl Jackson, was a young widow when I was a child. My two brothers and my sister had been born in the South, before my parents migrated to Michigan. I was the youngest daughter born at Herman Kiefer Hospital in November 1928. Our father, Curran Jackson, passed away at age 38 when I was four months old. Now my mother was rearing all of us and buying a house on the north end of town.

Many a time, when the county tax bill came due, my mother would take me with her to pay at the County Building. We would walk one block from our house on Cameron Street to Oakland, passing the Moore Elementary School (*Moore School of Observation*) on the way to the streetcar stop. We would wait there for the Oakland streetcar. As I recall, we never had to wait too long. The streetcar was manned by a driver who let us in the front door. Then, we could sit down in the front or go past the conductor who was stationed in the middle of the car. After paying our fare of 5 or 6 cents, we could sit in the rear of the streetcar until we reached our destination. In cold weather, those old streetcars would be filled with strong fumes which emanated from a heater that was located near the conductor or the driver.

My mother and I would get off the streetcar at Gratiot and Broadway and walk to the building on Randolph. After leaving the downtown area, the streetcar would meander along Adams to Hastings and another street or two before getting back to Oakland.

How exciting it was to ride down Hastings Street! The street was very well known. It was crowded from early morning until late at night. People were constantly going in and out of the flats where they lived. There were stores on the fronts of the buildings, all kinds of stores. There were grocery stores, dry goods stores, drug stores, poultry markets where live poultry could be purchased, killed, and cleaned. At the fish markets, live fish swam in huge steel tanks filled with water. Fish could be picked out for purchase as they swam by. The market owners would then scale the fish for their customers.

Whenever I am downtown and I pass the old County Building, I think of the pleasant times I had when I went with my mother to pay the county taxes.

Dorothy Kimble, a retired Detroit Public Schools Secretary, still lives in Detroit with her husband of 47 years, Sam Kimble. They have four daughters. This article was also published in Michigan Memories, Detroit Free Press, September 9, 1993.

Sophia's X-Ray Hair Shine
"Climax"
King Of Instant Hair Straighteners
Glendale 1820

L. G. W. RILEY
Distributor of
Sophia's Preparations and Hair Goods

253 E. Forest Ave.
Detroit Mich.
Ad from Colored Detroit

I Remember the J. L. Hudson's Store

by

Peggy A. Moore

HELPWANTED —SALES — FEMALE;
Apply in person on 12th Floor of J. L. Hudson Department Store

Back in the early 1950's when I was in my late teens, I answered an ad similar to the one pictured above. Remembering the things my homeroom teacher at CassTechnical High had drilled into her student's heads about applying for work, I made sure that I—

- Dressed neatly and conservatively
- Wore stockings with seams straight and contained no runs
- Wore low-heeled freshly polished shoes
- Carried a purse and wore hat and gloves
- Put just a whisper of a dab of cologne behind each ear

I really felt confident as I walked out of my parent's front door into the morning sunshine and boarded theWoodward streetcar downtown. The streetcar conductor let me off right in front of Hudson's Department Store. I entered the revolving doors and headed towards the elevator that would take me to the 12th floor where the Employment Department was located.

When the elevator operator stopped the car on the 12th floor and the gleaming brass doors swung open, I got off. High spirited, I headed toward a window that read "Employment Office." Other people had arrived there before me and had formed a long line. I took my place at the end and waited my turn.

Finally, I was the next to be waited on. I smiled pleasantly at the woman behind the glass window and told her I was there to apply for a job in sales.

"May I please have an application?" I asked. She took one hard look at me and immediately, her face turned into a hateful scowl from her forehead down to her chin. "Hudson's does not hire Negroes in sales," she spat out the words. To empathize her point, she tore up the form that would have gone to me, and threw it in a wastebasket. Then she looked around me, and began waiting on the next person in line.

Her actions frightened and embarrassed me. As I walked away in silence, I shook my head from side to side wondering why that lady with blond hair had said that to me. Didn't she realize that I had done exactly as that teacher at Cass had told me to do?

A sinking feeling came over me and I could feel hot tears on my cheeks as I took the escalator down rather than the elevator, hoping that by doing so, my racing heart would slow down a bit.

Growing up in Detroit in a all Negro close-knit neighborhood, my parents had shielded me from stark racism. Furthermore, at school, I was the student who always won the annual spelling bee, and I was always selected to play a lead role in plays. Why, by the time I was eleven years old, I participated in a weekly radio show on Station WJR. I also wrote for our school paper and was chosen Valedictorian of my graduation class.

My Canadian born and educated parent's spoke the Queen's English fluently and so did I. And I actually thought that "God Save The King" was America's national anthem, too. That was, until I entered kindergarten at five years old and learned better.

When the escalator reached the third floor I got off. I had decided to walk down the three remaining flights to the main floor. Automatically, I walked over to a table piled high with sale items. Very shortly, a saleslady came over to see if I wanted to purchase anything. "No, mam," I answered sadly as I took note of the fact that this saleslady spoke very bad English. One could barely understand what she was saying. And yet, the J. L. Hudson Co. had a policy back then that hired on the basis of skin color alone. My color was rich bronze — hers was chalk white.

You know... *I never forgot that incident.*

———

Ad from Colored Detroit

BILLY JACKSON
FUNERAL DIRECTOR
Full line of funeral equipments.
Refined Service.
Prices Agreeable
Phone Main 6621 Detroit, Mich.
332 Orleans St. No. 1700

Colchester, Ontario,

Saturday June 18, 1983

Dear Diary,

Today, I visited the actual place where my father, Theodore H. Moore was born. Stood on the corner of Harrison and Clitherow Streets in the spot where my father's family home stood when he was a boy.

Learned from old-timer, Clyde Scott, that this was all swamp land at one time. Rightfully this property is mine. It was legally left to the heirs of Theodore H. Moore. But somehow or other, his heirs lost claim due to a tax sale. Now, a stately home sits there where a white Canadian family resides.

Adjacent to this property is the property of my father's niece, Wavy Foster. Wavy's property rightfully came to her and she still has claim. Theodore moved up to Colchester together with Wavy's husband, Charlie.

Today is very warm and beautiful. I picked four pints of strawberries from a farm nearby. Charlie has a plot of land here where he plants vegetables.

Clyde Scott says he remembers my mother, Myrtle, well. Remembers her and her sister, Ida, as being real nice girls growing up. Clyde talked about how old Mr. Armstrong, the town preacher, would harness up his horse and buggy each Sunday morning to go to church.

Later in the day, a Jamacian woman dropped by. She told us that she worked for Dr. Posey who lived down the way. I learned also that my father's family home burned to the ground one afternoon. I notice, now, that a yellow fire plug sits where the family home once stood.

Dave Wolbert, my cousin from Windsor came by. He likes the Jamacian woman— really likes her a lot. So, he walks her home.

Bye,
Peggy A. Moore

Till We Meet Again

Your memoirs could be entitled,
"It's a Full Life."
Happiness, laughter,
struggles and strife.
Good times and bad times,
you faced them both the same.
Accepting all on life's terms,
never looking to place blame.
Sensitivity, wit,
charm, and finesse
Always upbeat,
sometimes more, never less.
"Grace Under Pressure"
is another good name.
A positive attitude
is your claim to fame.
Always energetic, sometimes
dynamic,
you explode onto the scene.
You give yourself completely or
not at all,
there is no in between.
Admired by some,
respected by all.
You're a "one-of-a-kind" kind of
guy.
This is the reason why,
It's so hard to say, *"Good-bye,"*
after-all....

(Written for Perry Moore upon his departure from this earth bound world)

COLORED DETROIT

DETROIT TRIBUNE
LEADING NEGRO WEEKLY OF MICHIGAN
Everybody's Newspaper
Only Negro Weekly
Owned, Edited & Printed In Detroit
2146 St.Antoine Phone Clifford 2934

FOR QUICK SALE

8 ROOMS & BATH $5,500; $600 DOWN.
2 FAMILY FLAT $6,500; $1,500 DOWN
7 ROOM COTTAGE $5,500; $500 DOWN
4 FAMILY BRICK FLAT; $28,500; $5,000 DOWN
2 FAMILY FLAT $9,000; $2,000 DOWN
JOHNSON & CLENNY
2323 St.Antoine St. Main 3390

Paradise Valley

They came
Hampton
The Duke
The Count
Earl
Ella
Pearl
and Joe too
They came
they saw
they sung
they played
and he fought
They sung the rapture
of eight bars at half-time
half-beat

and there was concrete cracking
shoe scrapping,
Cadillac Royal
Saturday night good times

and there was Sunday morning
finger popping, pew shouting,
foot stomping good times

and there was Monday morning
McDougal Street Blues
singing back to work times

and now it's gone
just the traces of smoke filled
memories remain

© 1997 Robert Haynes

Gray Ghetto

At dawn baffled brown birds
wing
Through subdued sun-rays
of the purple sky
Mocking twilight junkies
shooting up
In seedy galleries where many
recoil and die

Teen runaways, like flies,
Dispirited and appallingly blue
Sell their ravaged bodies for
crack and crusty crumbs
On which they anxiously chew

Through the concrete jungle
A myriad of faceless bodies
weave a bizarre tapestry
And on the toxic loom of aids,
with weathered fingers
Render the morbid essence of
their destiny

Uninhibited creatures — real
goners
Hang out on busy street corners
Having little else to do,
These Ghetto Rangers pander
strangers
For loose change to buy a cheap
brew

Natives cringe
At the blitz of hot guns
Above the howl of dogs sniffing
the odor
Of another day of chaos begun

The ruling class marching
through
Like legions of mechanical
soldiers
Impulsively glancing left to right
Over their tensed up shoulders

In living color, the media
Aggressively telecast
Overnight drive-by shooting, fire
bombing,
And looting of the underclass

Stressed out, choir robed souls
If asked by the press "Is this is
reality,"
Get a resounding "Yes! Yes!"
"Down here — dat's the way it
be!"

© 1998 James N. Ware

Submitted by Robert J. Haynes

Poor Ms. Maggie Smith

Poor Ms. Maggie Smith
She hasn't been the same since
her father died
She don't eat, don't sleep, don't
talk.
Nobody sees her anymore
She took care of him up until his
death.
Poor soul.
She loved that man.
She never took time out for
herself.
Constantly cared for him.
I knew it must have been rough
on her...
Working and all.
She never once complained.
Didn't seem to mind.
I would see her in the
super market
Always had a smile on her face
and a kind word for everyone.

Poor Ms. Maggie Smith
So young.
So sweet.
She lost her mother when she
was a baby
Never got married.
Never had the time.
Poor Ms. Maggie Smith
I wonder who she's for
Her father?
Or herself....

Nobody Told Her

She was the essence of beauty
as she strutted up the avenue
but, she didn't know
and nobody told her
Had eyes of Cleopatra
velvet skin of an ebony queen
I saw her wave, heard her yell
and I knew she didn't know
Straightness of her spine told the story
certainly she was a descendant of royalty
I heard the clicking of her stilettoed heels
and I knew she didn't know
Bejeweled sweat-band hugged her head
and nobody told her it was really a crown
I saw her lean into a strange car's window
and I knew she didn't know
Black motherhood
hung heavily in her breasts
generations of kings
dwelled in her swaying hips
I heard...
"Only twenty dollars, sugar"...
slide from her lips
and I knew she didn't know
Pity — men crawled in and out of her life
every night
and they never even cared that she was of a
royal breed
I saw her head toss back
in wild laughter
as the car tore from the curb
I knew she didn't know
She didn't know —
and nobody told her so....

SECTION III – THE PEOPLE

ADAMS STREET

Angeline Eastland & Blanche Woods - *Submitted by Elvenia McCowin*

Fannie Davis Boone — *Submitted by Karen Williams*

Courtesy of Jacqueline Caffey Collection

Courtesy of Jacqueline Caffey Collection

Sisters

Sisters stick together
like coagulated blood,
clotting up the tight
parameters of a
thick and muddy
existence.
Sisters practice
a religion
based on ritual
passed on by their mothers
from their spittle
and hot breath.
CPR is necessary
for continuation
of the species.

© 1997 Teresa Tucker Moore

Submitted by Mamie Montgomery

Beautiful

Yes, keep in mind
I am beautiful
I am wonderful, intelligent,
and true...

I don't need special attention
but I do require equality
I am not trying to make
a lot of noise
but I won't be told to hush
or to be quiet

I'm not trying to cut
to the front of the line
but I won't go to the back,
either.

When I hurt inside
There is no place to hide
I can't go right,
because there is nothing
left.
There is only down
because up is too much
of a challenge.
I have to fight every step
of the way
Yet, I am to blame,
when I become lost.

Yes, keep in mind
I am beautiful
I laugh at tragedy,
I smile at pain
I cheer away
misfortune that bring
thunder and rain

I represent all that's
wonderful
and joyous to mankind
it's all in the beauty of
love,
and very easy...
to find.

© 1997 Quontina Moore

Street Life

Neon lights flashing in the night
saying move ahead
Street-walkers, ladies of the night
anxiously awaiting payment in
full

Johns cursing
with pictures of daughters,
sons, and wives tucked safely
in wallets.
Soft dreams,
soft thoughts never fade

Open until 2 am
liquor and wine to sell
Bar-B-que chicken and ribs
odors drifting on the wind
above the neon lights

Movement abounds
stirring life to the fullest
no regrets, no promises made
only summer nights
a few words spoken
nothing said

©1997 Crystal Moore

Submitted by Mamie Montgomery

Submitted by Evelyn Rhodes

Mildred Winder
Submitted by Sandra Miller

Too Soon

As I gaze out my window
At other girls my age
Inside my bloated belly
A fire begins to rage

I watch their young hips swaying
As to a silent drum
And tall young boys trail them
Wolf-calling and eyeing their
forms

The girls flash a knowing glance
Heads tossing quick and high
Silent drums keep pounding
Their fiery fervors intensify

Beating out the tune
"I'm looking for a love"
They sing a song I once felt
A song I once knew of

I found a love, a special love
He made me feel real grown
Now, I'm with child and love's
not here
Love left me all alone

I try to smile a pleasant smile
And try to understand
How I became a woman so
soon
When he wanted to be a
man....

For fourteen-year-old mothers everywhere

© 1984 Dianne White-Morris

Days Like This

On days like this
I think of you
And wonder if
You're lonely too.

I need your touch
Your tender kiss.
When I'm alone
On days like this.

I pray that destiny
will decree
More glorious days
For you and me.

Then no longer must
I just reminisce
Apart from you
On days like this.

© 1997 Jewel Martin

Love Passage

In radiant rays of pastel light
Flowering love explodes
In passions bright.
Ghostly shadows dare not
gather
But flee self-pity's nest and
scatter.

Love relishes the heart like
Day's dawn effervescent breath,
And champions over
Life's weathered weft.

In passion and bliss,
She is crowned
Her voice raised high
In silent sounds.

Love scales the mind's forest
Of backyard fences
Like sterling rays of sunshine.
Rejuvenates a dozing soul
With fruits succulent and
divine.

Love lends audience
To sobbing nightingale's
Broken hearts so tender.
But cannot silence
The oceans of pain
Lest the soul remembers.

Garfield Lounge, 1955— L to R. Beatrice Buck, Rosita Sims, & Anita Carswell. *Courtesy of Beatrice Buck Collection*

Ladies Having Fun, 1959 — L. to R., Etta Jones, Beatrice Buck, Catherine Norman, Gwen Jones, Thelma Pye, Pam Ransom, Ann Wilson, Lena Webster, Catheryne Fowler.
Courtesy of Beatrice Buck Collection

Miss Emma and Mr. Man

Things hadn't been right
between them
since far back as I can remember.
No morning pleasantries like
most married couples
who've been together that long.

Shoot, they didn't even sleep
together.
She cooked her food...
He cooked his.

After all they had been through
with them white folks down
south,
you'd think they'd be tight
as new shoes.
Their glares were hard
and cold as steel.

I believe there was real passion
between them... at one time.
But now, the only thing real
between them
was DISGUST and ANGER.

"Daddy, would you rather die or
kiss mama," I'd ask,
knowing that surely he would
rather kiss my grandmother!
"Neither one,"
he would coldly reply.

When mama got sick and died,
He grieved mightily.
I remember his hands
rubbing her face
and looking at her in the casket
as if he were searching
for something,
or trying to remember what it
felt like to touch her.
And who was Mr. Blaylock?!
(*The subject of many arguments!*)

Some say, the white folks took
daddy's house away from him
and we all had to come
up north to live.

I guess I'll never know
what really happened
between them.
I'll never know the
pain,
humiliation and
suffering they endured.

I'll never know the
evilness that destroyed
their love ,
or why they were so
disappointed with
each other.

But I know that I loved
them both desperately,
and that God forgives
them
for whatever mistakes
they made.
So sad... they couldn't
forgive each other.

© 1997 Evelyn Phosia Holmes

Courtesy of Jacqueline Caffey Collection

Measured Love

If your love,
in all its categories,
were an anchor,
I might be weighted down
by its bulk

If your love
were layered upon me like
muslin,
the cotton would be too
coarse,
too abrasive.

You see, what I need from
you
is love that has tight fingers
with a loose grip.

© 1997 Teresa Tucker Moore

George Moore's Parents, Bernice & Jim Taylor in Lobby of the Pryor Hotel - *Submitted by Peggy A. Moore*

Conjured Dream

When we met
You were like a breath
of fresh air
And I thought you were
awakening me
From a long slumber
I looked into your eyes,
Dark pools of intrigue
I thought I saw them
Flicker with interest.
You spoke my name,
Soft and plaintive
I thought you were saying
I could be the one.
You touched me
Playfully and modestly
I thought I felt
The passion of my youth
The Lion of my past.
So, I lit a candle
Opened my heart
So that you could see clearly
The soul of me therein.
You laughed
Bubbles of giggles
Spilling forth like foam
Mocking and chilling
Suddenly, in the distance
I heard thunder
So I closed my pain
Put on my slicker
And headed for the rain.
Too bad....

ST. ANTOINE ST.

Peggy & George Moore, Sunnie Wilson's Bar, 1953

Submitted by Peggy A. Moore

Submitted by Brenda McGee

Mamie & Earl Montgomery
Submitted by Mamie Montgomery

Mamie Montgomery
by
Evelyn Holmes

Mamie Washington moved to Detroit, Michigan from Savannah, Georgia over fifty years ago. She married the late Earl A. Montgomery who moved to Detroit from Lexington, Mississippi. They lived in Detroit for more than fifty years. First on Adams street, then Euclid, and lastly, on Woodward and Stimson.

Earl Montgomery operated the *Victory Social Club* on St. Antoine and Gratiot for many years and retired from the Kingsley Inn, in Bloomfield Hills, Michigan. Mamie worked at the Hotel Tuller on Adams and Park.

Earl and Mamie enjoyed a full social life in Detroit, patronizing the various Night Clubs in the Hastings Street and downtown Jefferson area.

Mr. Montgomery & Two Lovely Ladies - *Submitted by Mamie Montgomery*

Someone Special

Someone special
Came into my life
He said he loves me
Wants me to be his wife
He's so sweet
And kind to me
Now that we are together
I feel complete.

Someone special
Danced with me all night
The way he held me in his arms
It felt so right
He opens doors for me
Pulls out my seat
Makes me feel like a lady
Now, isn't that neat.

Someone special
Gave me some *money*
Told me
I know you need it, honey
He said I love you,
I'm here if you need me
When he said that to me
I just couldn't believe it.

Someone special
Looked into my eyes
Pulled out a ring
Oh! What a surprise
Said, Hey, baby
I'm in love with you
All I want to hear you say
Are the words — I DO

© 1997 Teresa M. Brown

The Lost Valley

Each year, it's the same
it seems by now
I would know
that you are gone

Yet , here I am again
waiting, wanting,
needing... you

Anticipating
your effervescent smile
your warm caress
your kiss
that promise of more
to come

Paradise Valley
My *raison d'etre* .
Where are you?....

Translation - *raison d'etre*:
French for - *reason for being*

© 1997 Barbara L. Hunter

Mrs. Alberta Henderson (left) & Church Members - *Submitted by Karen Williams*

Time

Time can not diminish
The joy you have given to me
Nor can it cool the warmth I feel
With each sweet memory.

Time can not transform
The beauty in you I see
Nor can it fade your light which shines
For all the world to see.

Time can only enhance
The closeness that we share
And remind us of the trying times
When together, we were there.

Time will bring to closing
The passage of our years
So while I have the time I'll say:
I love you, my sweet dear.

© 1997 Dianne A. Rhodes

Inside Out

(A Cry For Life)

Why are you so
bitter
Angry
Afraid ?

All those around
you
You attempt to
make
Miserable
Because
You
Are
You treat life as if
it were a curse
Not with drink
Nor drug
Do you find solace
For reality
Creeps
In-between the
highs

Come with me
If you dare
Disrobe
Stand naked before me
As I with you
Embrace me

Your bitter kiss will become
Seasoned and sweet
Your anger will succumb to
pleasure
Fear... will not have a place
Within your heart
For happiness
Will have rented all of the rooms
I offer you
Paradise on earth
Welcome, baby
To Paradise Valley
Home...
Where you are always
... welcomed

© 1997 Barbara L. Hunter

Love Speaks

They are very different,
the two of them...
He is tall and lean
with a young, agile, athletic body.
She is short with a
certain soft roundness.

His dark hair thrives with moisture,
Thick curls grow tight around
his handsome, almost boyish
face.
Her thin hair grows straighter in
time,
Accenting her round, full face.

He is morning.
She is night.
He is dusty Southern country
roads.
She, a Northern city, concrete
and steel.
He is quiet, almost introspective.
She is impulsive.
He listens and responds quietly.
She talks too much.
He is disciplined with food
Drink and exercise.
She gratifies her
senses too much.
He is Black.
She is White.
He is morning.
She is night....

© 1994 Mary Ann Sestili

Pain

It's over. No more agonizing
thoughts.
Our love failed...
Time worked against us.
A feeling is dragging you to light
a-jaxing what we shared.

I did not lose.
1 don't have your picture.
Like Kodak snapshots
there is no change.
The way you held your head
to the left,
rearranging that clinical mind,
sorting early Christmas presents,
dusting portraits,
ruffling pages, being you.

I can't wish you love,
I've tried.
God, I tried.
You understand, I'm sure.
It was the same when I lost Sam.
I thought I wanted another cat
but the pain was constant.
I never told you, but I cried
when Sam died.
I felt lost.
Not cheated. Lost.

It's sad that your poem
should come now.
Should be
whatever it is...
Saying so little....

All my tears

All the tears
That I shed from my face,
How easily they flow
Drops of pain
Liquid sorrow.
Oh, how they sting
Like the salts of the sea
Trapped in my wounds
Aching to be free.
These tears, I cry
Must run their course
Just as the river
Flows back to its source.
Just like the river
These tears, I cry
They cleanse my soul
Watering my dreams,
My thirst for life.

I, too,
Like the river
Will stand
The test of time.

Intimate Praise Of Beauty

Running wild and free
through the chambers of my
mind
The wind blows a silent
sweet whisper of passion on my
cheek
I feel the rays of the sun stinging
the brown velvet skin of my back
as I lay naked next to my man
embraced by his strong and
forceful arms
Protecting me from all harm

The silent hours of night
have drifted into the break of
dawn
I awake to find this beautiful
Prince of Darkness lying naked
in my presence
My heart begins to beat
faster than a roaring tide
My black smooth skin starts to
sweat
My eyes are filled with love
and devotion to this sensuous
spirit of my heart

He turns the opposite way
making it possible for me
to have sight of his long and
masculine back
his round and firm buttocks
and his miraculously smooth
even thighs
Oh, how I would love
to cup them up in my hand
and drink the potion of eternal
ecstasy

But for now...
I must be very quiet
my thoughts are becoming loud
and might awaken my love
Sleep well, my Prince....

Moon Glow

It is cold here,
and deathly quiet.
The only sound I hear
is the beating of my heart.
My breath clouds my window.
But, out in the distance
beyond the tops of the buildings
and barren cotton wood trees,
I see the moon.
And it is this sight that I behold
wishing that you would
step out your door
at this precise moment in time
so that its light may touch you
with its magic as it has touched
me.
So that you will know how
deeply I care.
So that we may be joined in its
glow
if only for a moment.
No matter, how long...
No matter, how brief....

Submitted by Minnie Brogdon

Submitted by Minnie Brogdon

Lost

When she was a girl
she had visions and dreams
But when she grew up
she began to do bad things.
She dropped out of school
and ran away
No one in her family knows
where she is today.
I last saw her on Woodward
talking with her pimp
I could tell he was beating her,
she walked with a limp
Wounds on her skin
from poisonous injections
Once a beautiful girl,
now a ghastly reflection
Her dreams and visions
have floated away
Her body sick
and wretched with decay
A family with nothing left to do
but hope and pray.
Now she roams abandoned
streets.
Spends all her money getting
high
Wishing someday
she'll learn how to fly
Fly away from all her troubles
the hurting and the pain
Wanting things to change
and never be the same.
Asking God to forgive her sins
While still taking
poisonous medicine within
A discouraged women child
who did not find her way
Gave the Lord, Jesus Christ
her life...
yesterday.

© *1997 Jamila Kafi (Age 14)*

Lonely Dawn

The day dawns clear
Without a cloud
And my thoughts clamor
Almost aloud.
As I sit and think and reminisce
Of a glance, a smile, a touch, a
kiss
Of quiet times and hours of bliss
Together with you on days like
this.
If the fates are smiling from
above
Why must I be without my love?
So knowing faith, I do foresee
That soon my love will be with
me.
So I'll not shed a single tear
For soon I know that you'll be
near
To share our destined time of
bliss
When we're alone on days like
this.

© *1997 Jewel Martin*

8 Ball In Side Pocket

Soft Side of Hastings, Oakland
Avenue,
Wilfred's Billiard Parlor jammed
between
The Pig Bar-B-Q and the Echo
Theatre.

Slick Herman chalks his cue with
resolution,
Blue powder whispers to the
floor.
He misses an easy bank shot in
the corner.

Safe Eddie would always leave
you on the rail
Or hidin' behind balls you didn't
want to shoot.
And steady Jerome looks for non-
believers.
Hasn't missed a bank shot in four
days.

Silent Ambrose shoots 9-ball with
Ralph, the Merchant.
Ralph accuses Silent of moving
his balls for a better angle,
Calls Silent a name.

Silent flashes quicker-than-light
Two inches of switch-blade to
Merchant's jugular.
In the stop-stillness of the mo-
ment,
You could hear a rat piss on
cotton.

"Don't you ever call me that ...
ever."

Silent wins the 9 ball game by
forfeit.
Merchant can't find a cue that
will sit still in his hand.

Earl Montgomery & his boys enjoying a game of pool - *Submitted by Mamie Montgomery*

Doesn't look like pool, but Earl & his boys are enjoying something - *Submitted by Mamie Montgomery*

Mamie & Earl Montgomery (Standing in center) entertaining some of their close friends - *Submitted by Mamie Montgomery*

Courtesy of Jacqueline Caffey Collection

Baby Ray

Baby Ray cribbed on the
blacktop streets of Detroit
Scratched high honors at Southeastern.
His folks left for Vegas to make it big.

"Someone To Watch Over Me,"
Which he used to hum all the time.
Won't you tell her, please
to put on some speed?

We used to call him "Mooch" cause
he was always on "E" — not anymore.
Raymond found the fast lane.
His street cabinet helped.

Wolf, the Con Man for all seasons,
Fast-break Benjamin always in foul trouble.
Bee, her dime-sized waist and healthy hips,
Stu the Police Advisor,
Phil the Soothsayer of John R.

Early mornings — Pindillys to play 21.
If the cards fell right
All hustlers in the joint got gappers.
A fresh start tomorrow.

The Cakewalk Shuffle to the Frolic
Where Arnett Cobb was working out.
The Garfield Lounge for chicken in the basket.
If action was still acting,
On to Sassy Sarah at the Flame.

Courtesy of Jacqueline Caffey Collection

Courtesy of Richard Thomas Collection

Submitted by Mamie Montgomery

Submitted by Mamie Montgomery

Submitted by Mamie Montgomery

A Detroiter Like Me

I like warm nights, bright stars,
fine wine, good food, and love.
I like the morning sun,
a pleasant smile,
the laughter of a small child,
a refreshing shower, and Happy Hour.

I like CNN, the old WJZZ,
WCHB Channel 56 and WDET,
The Learning Channel and Discovery,
HBO, Cinemax, Showtime and BET (Sometimes).

I like things to fix, magic tricks,
smiling faces and going places;
Stephen King, diamond rings,
and I like THINGS.

I like fine art, most movies
and some movie stars,
small talk, and making decisions.
But I don't care much for politicians.

I like good books, computers,
and adult toys and games,
DIA, a fine play,
and quiet walks in the park.

I like stimulating conversation,
and a good massage,
taking pictures, telling jokes,
and making people laugh.

I like dancing, holding hands,
talking, dreaming, planning
and making love.

I like a lot of things
I don't do very well
like playing the piano,
golf, checkers, chess,
and drawing pictures.

I like things I do a little better,
like making wine,

playing the clarinet
and saxophone,
and being alone.

I like to cook most anything,
and I like to eat.
I like steak at the Boardroom.

I like escargot, caviar,
lobster, most seafood,
except squid,
and I like chittlins,
candied yams,
greens and most soul food
except sweetbread.

I like Absolute Vodka Martinis
dry, with anchovy olives,
and I like Genessee Cream Ale
at the Soup Kitchen Saloon.

I miss the 1940 Chop House,
Mr. "T's," and The 10 Gentlemen.
I like eating out at Mr. Mike's
and Pegasus;
breakfast at the New Detroiter,
lunch at Edmund's Place and
Lilli's anytime.

I like the Whitney, Opus One,
Van Dyke Place and the St. Regis,
when I can.
I like to laugh and knowing
I can cry if I want to.

And...
I like to win and
knowing its OK if I don't
I like animals and the great
outdoors
and I like fresh air
I like believing in a Supreme
Being
and the comfort in believing
He or She is out there
somewhere....

I like small things and tall things
and gentle things and quiet
things.
I like good friends
although they are few
and I like new friends.
I like ME and I Like YOU.

© 1997 Reginald H. Gibbs

Million Man March

October 16, 1995

To be chanted to the tune of "By Our Love"

And they will know you are
black men by your stride
by your stride...
And they will know you are
black men by your stride
by your stride...
And you'll know they are
black men by their pride...
And you'll know that I am
spiritually by your side
by your side...

Marchin' on past the naysayers
Marchin' on past our divisions
Pass on by the nitpickers...
Pass on by the excuses...
They will know you are
black men by your love...
by your love...
They will know you are
black men by your love
for your brother...
They will know you are
black men by your respect
for each other...

They will know you are
black men by your pride...
by your pride

© 1997 Rain Africa Reign

Robert Williams - *Submitted by Geraldine Metoyer*

Jessie & Louise Ware, couple on right enjoy an evening of entertainment at The El Sino. *Submitted by James N. Ware*

George Slayton, Dr. Pharr C. Freeman, Sr., Jessie P. Slayton & James Heard at the Three Sixes 666 — *Submitted by Hilda Vest*

Hilda Vest & Brother, Pharr at Belle Isle. *Submitted by Hilda Vest*

Anna Goodspeed, a friend, Jewel & Bill Launchie at Three Sixes - *Submitted by Reginald Gibbs*

Another Three Sixes Party 666 - Left to Right —Mary Gray, Pharr C. Freeman, Jr. and Mrs. Mattie Blance Freeman — *Submitted by Hilda Vest*

Elegy for Jeanne

She never shared secrets
Only her mirrors
which transformed
Acned youth

Grins broke our harmony
On *Bad Bad Whiskey*
As her voicing and mine
Moved in and out of tune

Sandwiches in her mama's
kitchen
Made us choke
On laughter
and peanut butter

Old photographs
offered no warning
Her smile
was stowed-away sadness

I do remember
her fear of guns
I do recall her reserve

When did
she lose her fear
Where did
she get her nerve

Another Colored Girl

(For ntozake shange)

he waz slow to speak
but she caught his smile
and ignored the ache
it caused inside her
"where you been," she asked
with the stare of a prosecuting
attorney
"been waitin' since three"
he stood closer now
his shoulders falling over her
like a wave off the atlantic

she had welcomed him
between her thighs but once
and waz billed nine months by
the piper
three she had paid already
along w/tips she said each
morning
when the rush of vomit
awakened her
"we spoze to see the doctah,
you know
So's i can get outta this
this mess i've gotten in"

marvin reached in his pocket
past his wallet,
under his house key
and pulled out a wad
big as ali's fist
"you can get on with
success now
but before you go i gotta ask
did you listen to me that night
i told you then
i'm tellin' you now
i need a woman
to be my storm and my sun
to be the condition of
the rainbow
we both gotta see
besides, wouldn't our love
be a complement to a child"

the question went unanswered
as she hurried past the
horn player
on to the cleavers
that would cut away her burden
and kill marvin's heir

COLORED DETROIT

Skinny Legs and Old Cars

If you are a person with skinny
legs,
Be glad you have legs at all.
If they move, it seems rather
irrelevant
That they happen to be sort of
small.
You should he proud of your
skinny legs,
And think that your legs are great,
If they can propel you back and
forth,
While supporting your body
weight.
Oh, you might desire a fuller leg,
A shapelier calf, or a cuter shin.
But thank God you have those
skinny legs,
In whatever shape they're in.

You might be driving an older car,
In need of a few repairs.
But what do you care if the car is
old,
As long as it gets you there?
Cause everyone wants a new car
That's loaded, and shiny and nice;
But remember the payments on
that new car,
And its owner must pay the price.

If you can't afford a new car,
There's no need to fall apart,
Cause when you turn the switch
on the son -of-a-bitch,
You simply want it to start!
So walk proudly on those skinny
legs,
And lean when you drive your old
car,
Cause skinny legs and old cars
Have carried many a person far!

Black Eden

By

Josephine H. Love

A few months ago I stumbled across the enclosed snapshots, taken with a first camera during an unforgettable experience of my early adolescent years. It was a late 1920's motor trip with my parents across the northern tip of Michigan's Lower Peninsula and south to Benton Harbor and St. Joseph.

Memorable features of that journey were the state's lovely woodland areas and vast stretches of cherry orchards. We picked freely from inviting crops of berries enroute to the fascinating vacation colonies of Baldwin and Lake counties: Idlewild and Woodland. We vacationed in one and visited the other over a period of several days.

Idlewild was known as "*Black Eden*," "*Apollo of the North*" or "*Black Las Vegas*." Its cottages were owned and rented by African-Americans from many cities as far west as Chicago and St. Louis. They had invested in the resort potential of lovely lakefront, woodland and contingent properties during the second decade of the century.

Woodland, a short distance away, was a serene, far less exciting companion resort. Both represented unique investments of African-American capital. Visitors came from many parts of the country. Today's traffic has lessened, but the loyalty of property owners remains into the third and fourth generations of family ownership.

Our purpose in going there was to inspect plots of land acquired sight unseen some years before by my father's mother. We also wanted to visit family friends. Our hosts were Hazel Harrison, the outstanding black concert pianist of the day, and her mother, Olive. Ms. Harrison was the first musician trained entirely on American soil to be invited to appear as soloist with a major European orchestra. In 1904, she had performed as guest artist with the Berlin Philharmonic. She was invited to return to Germany and study with composer-pianist Feruccio Busoni.

Upon the adjacent waterfront property was the summer cottage built and owned by Charles Chestnut, an early 20th Century novelist from Cleveland. Various notables were familiar figures, many of them considered legendary today as writers, historians, civic leaders, politicians and business people. They visited not only for pleasure and relaxation but to participate in public forums and lecture series. It was, metaphorically speaking, a *"Black Chatauqua,"* located in the Midwest.

Fishing, swimming, and canoeing were the traditional pastimes. In addition, there was lively entertainment: nightclubs, dance halls, and — I am sure — discreet gambling. Shows featured Can-Can and American Vaudeville Acts managed by TOBA, official acronym for a Theater Owners Association, but referred to with tongue-in-cheek sarcasm as *"Tough on Black Acts."* That referred to the deplorable backstage housekeeping in segregated venue, mostly white owned, that were the only outlets available to black entertainers of the day.

In the near future, I hope to revisit the site of that long-ago experience which left an impressionable teenager with a sense of what could be accomplished through spirited community effort in the face of disheartening social conditions. I expect to be stirred in much the same way.

Josephine Harold Love lives in Detroit and is Director of **"Your Heritage House."**

Joe Ann & Jiam Desjardins — enjoying the beach at Idlewild's Flamingo Club - *Courtesy of Jiam Desjardins*

Some of Mamie & Earl Montgomery's vacation photos taken at different resorts around the country

Dog Days

A Poem for Idlewilders

— In wildness is the
preservation of the world.
Henry David Thoreau

Summer in Black Eden:
woven carpets of sweetbriar,
growing fat and free on
conversation,
hickory-smoked short ribs,
soaring heat of Sirius,
a righteous r and r.
Listening to Basie, Eckstine,
Domino,
cast iron pots of corn-mealed
perch sizzling,
we would lean on cool,
double-humped rocks
letting the sun paint our cells
a warm rich brown,
as we swat squitos,
the arms of shy crushes
chasing lanterns of fireflies
across the warm, ink land.

Idlewild—
2,000 acres of cool green weeds,
white-washed cabins,
Memorial to Labor Day
picnics in culture and pride,
visitors from Vegas,
the Boardwalk
and Apollo,
walking proudly like lions,
shaking laughter from our
manes.

© *1996 Karen Williams*

This Small World

The World grows smaller every-
day,
A looming submarine
Wisdom low, and water high,
A life to live, where each shell
dies,
All submerged in "We" and
"They,"
And newborn minds, a field to
play,
So young, *confused,* when
friendships end,
Yes, far too young for arrogance,
Living, breathing, purging
growth,
And brand-new knowledge—
Cultural.
This world a vessel of pride and
fear,
And labeled human beings,
Living, breathing, always sharing,
Common little things—
Food, space, water, air,
Fire, birth, and some despair.
Yet, people grow, and wisdom
knows,
As sure as sun does shine,
As sure as day will greet the
night,
Hello, will meet good-bye.
And as surely as we live and
breathe,
As our Knowledge grows,
Truth, and peace of mind
emerge,
To anchor this small, small
world....

© *1996 Marie A. Berry*

The Umbrella

I wish I had known you
When you were but a wee boy
Your hair long, in big black curls
Your skin, the color of
Coffee and cream
Smooth as velvet.
Perhaps, we could have ran
Through fields of wild flowers
And Black-eyed Suzies
Chased each other with sticks
You pulling at my long plaits
Laughing at my flower sack dress
And matching bloomers
Perhaps, we could have shared
A peanut butter and jelly
sandwich
Or sat together
at the school movies
In a hot, humid Gym
Warmed by a Louisiana sun
Or helped me catch lightning
bugs
At sundown and put them in jars.
Perhaps, you could have
buttoned
My high-top shoes that were
forever
Flopping open as I ran through
The clover, St. Augustine, Touch
Me Nots, and Shame Face grass
Near the fig trees
In Mama Dora's yard.
Perhaps, we could have helped
Each other up each time we fell
Kissed each others bruises
And made them well
Played house,
Me the mommy, you the daddy
Perhaps, fate could have brought
Us together sooner
But instead, she waited
And sent you along one
Rainy afternoon at the
University overlooking the
Mighty Mississippi
You asked,
"May I share your umbrella."
You know, I thank God
I had an umbrella to share.
Through the years,
It has weathered many a storm
Now... it's a little tattered,
A little worn
Even so, it still continues
To keep us huddled together,
Arm in arm, Close, ...and dry.

© *1997 Geraldine Metoyer*

Effers Broadus (number 4 from left, standing) -*Submitted by Michael Tolliver*

A Party In The Valley - *Submitted by Mamie Montgomery*

Effers Broadus (Top Row, number 7 from left) - *Submitted by Michael Tolliver*

Smooth Character

Camel like in style carrying
His own water
He is able to travel by night
Without the benefit of light.

Smooth Character
Sheds all emotions,
Done with crying
Getting ready for dying

Smooth Character
High upon a board
Facing situations fearless,
Unafraid
and...
always late.

© *1997 Crystal Moore*

Internment

Shame
holding your head like that
your flag half mast
Who's dead
you ain't

Why can't you take hold
and know that life's
not a lying-in-state time
It's a gittin' up
celebratin' time

Raise your flag
black man
Proclaim your own spirit
your own energy
your own holiday

Emancipate your own self
goddammit
Time's wastin'
and your woman
waits...

© *1993 Hilda Vest*
Selection from "Sorrow's End," Broadside Press

A Social Gathering of Paradise Valley Society Ladies *Submitted by Peggy A. Moore*

Awakening

On the wings of time,
I have traveled through life
searching for that one true thing,
that special someone
to brighten up my days
and cause my heart to sing.

Down through the years,
I have never encountered
a heart so pure and fair.
But through your warmth
and tenderness of soul,
I find you special and rare.

The ray of light on your face
is as fresh as the dawn,
Your eyes glisten like dew,
and I cannot imagine
a love such as this
not being shared with you.

The soothing sound
of your voice
calms my fears,
until at last,
my fears are gone.
For in your arms
I find a peace and security
from which I will never roam.

The gentleness of your touch
makes my heart quiver with joy
as your sweetness
draws me within.
For you are the reason
I can smile
when I say that my journey
has finally come...
to an end.

© 1997 Latres Orr

Corine Fletcher's (Right Rear) Ladies Club - *Submitted by Jeanette Vaughn*

Phillip Greene - *Submitted by Karen Williams*

Submitted by Mamie Montgomery

Gloria & Harold Broden's Wedding - *Submitted by Peggy A. Moore*

Jacqueline & Leroy Caffey - *Courtesy of Jacqueline Caffey Collection*

Twenty-Fifth Wedding Anniversary

You were with me in
the transition
when I shed the sashes
of girlhood
and fashioned womanly belts
You were with me
One Sunday long ago
we abducted the ocean's scent
through windows of a narrow
church
and made promises each to the
other

Submitted by Mamie Montgomery

You were with me

We invaded the beaches of
Monterey
never certain though of the
captors
Was it me
was it the ocean's song
or was it you
the cowry of my universe
You courted me long dis-
tance
your fantasies safe
in flag-striped envelopes
The mailman never knew
the intimacy of his delivery
Then one day your gift,
a beutiful black pearl, arrived
never to return to its bed
in Japan
You could not hear me swear
that it matched the pearl grow-
ing in my belly
The roses you planted still bloom
and spill hopelessly across
fences and borders in gardens
where our children played
in seasons of their youth

Now, when we are weekend
winos
stumbling and speaking in
tongues
I recall that you administered my
first drink
being certain of its potency
Your watchful guard was
anxious, yet gentle
I grew silly before your eyes
and came to rest and
to be born again
in your arms
You confide that you like my
laughter
so I leave it un-canned on your
nightstand
and hope that it will temper
your sleep
We make love now,
not always out of lust
but out of good habits acquired
Like warm baths at the end of
crowded days
or windows pushed open
after rain

© 1993 Hilda Vest
Selection from "Sorrow's End," Broadside Press

Look To Heaven

It's been a while
the nights are lonely
and I can't seem to find
the moments that we shared.
Yet, if you look to Heaven
by mid-night
wherever I am, your glare
like moonlight
will fall from the stars
through my window pane
down and across my pillow
and cast your shadow
next to me.
Cruel are the memories
the thoughts you left behind
knowing nothing can compare
wanting to be there.
But, if you look to Heaven by
noon
I can forever stand before the
sun
feeling the warmth of your day
tasting its breeze upon my lips
traveling south to hug my chest
then riding freely
at the hem of my dress.
Life has mountains, valleys,
and streams
none are more apart than we.
Yet, they face the Heavens
and find a way to bond.
So, if there ever is a storm
in your world
then look to Heaven, my love,
I'll catch your tears
as they fall from the sky
collect them in my jar
and hold them forever close
to my heart....

© 1995 Sandra Ann Chambers

Love's Embrace

My pink satin nightgown
covered with perfume,
mixed with my body heat
scents up the room
I've waited all day
for you to come home,
I've waited all night
for us to be alone.

I need your smile,
your warmth, your touch.
I need to express that
I love you so much.
My heart is like butter
that melts in your hand,
as I'm held in the arms
of you, my sweet man.

I do not know why
I love you like I do.
But one thing I do know,
there's no life without you
My pink satin nightgown
still covered with perfume,
with hopes that you, my love
will be here soon....

© 1997 Latres Orr

Elvenia & Eulac McCowin's Wedding
Submitted by Elvenia McCowin

These Hands

They were not hands that would
win a Jergen's lotion commercial
These were hands that picked
cotton, hoed fields,
drew well water
These were hands that would
spread out over a bible's pages
as though *The Word* would seep
in through the fingers

These were hands that,
with a touch
could soothe a fever
could give strength
could give comfort
could give chastisement
deliver love

These were hands that were
usually covered with flour
frying chicken,
or with grease to shine little
"ashy" legs
many times holding a dustrag
or a mop

These were hands that
did a man's job in Ford's Plant
to raise her children
to help raise her
children's children
and her children's
children's children

These hands, once
strong and enduring,
now still
Finally adorned with
the long nails
always wished for
That grew when the
hands had not the
strength to do the
many things
so accustomed to
doing
Long, slender,
holding a red rose
In repose

These hands are what I will
always remember
When I remember love
When I remember comfort
When I remember you, *Mama*

© 1998 Sandra Miller

——————

You

I know we just met
but I feel I've known
you all my life.
Seems like you've crossed my
path before
maybe once, maybe twice.

There's something about your
ways
that I can't help but love.
When I'm around you,
my heart flies
like a happy white dove.

When you touch me
I get the warmest feeling
And even though
I haven't given it to you
my love is what you're stealing.

When you speak,
your words are like
a flowing river of passion.
Pulled under by the currents,
I feel myself crashing.

I'm drowning
in the deep end of your love
And just when I think
I need help,
I just look above.
And there you are
smiling down on me
Because you knew
if I tried your love
I would never, never be free

© 1997 Michanda Gant (Age 14)

My Love

Every time I see you
I wonder if we could ever be.
If I could ever love you
and you could love me.
When we first met
I never thought that I'd feel this
way.
And those feelings grow more
and more
the longer they stay.
When we're together
I try to play that nonchalant
game,
But let me tell you, the way I feel
and the way I act,
will never, never
be the same.

Like Magic

He picked flowers from air
made birds and scarves
appear like magic
and she could never tell
the cards he would be holding
His hands were quicker
than her eyes
and he had magic up his sleeves
It fueled her fascination

He was magnet for her metal
A master of illusion,
he snatched the cloth
from her table
and didn't break a single dish
He was a sorcerer
who had her mesmerized,
until his sleight of hand
got slightly out of hand

He pulled her heart
out of his hat,
sawed it in half
and disappeared
in a puff of smoke
like magic...

Selection from "Wine Sip" Broadside Press

Disgusted

I waited for you
And what did you do?
You played with my emotions
Caused a comotion.
I fell for you so god damn fast
Thinking your love would stay
and last.
Told me how much you care
That you'd always be there.
Said your love would never die
But I soon found out that was
just a lie.
If you wanted me for you
Then you would've proved that
Your love was true.
By asking me to be yours
And letting everyone know
Instead you chose to keep me a
secret
Locked behind the door.
Treated me
like I was something on the side
And you could come to me
Anytime you decide
Now, I'm sorry
I have to bust your bubble
You can only have one
Two — you got trouble.

Mable

I told you Mable,
but I told you wrong
I said that by Christmas,
I'd be back home
Lord knows I been trying,
both begging and lying,
but something keeps holding me
strong
Something, I just can't put my
hands on.

Believe me Mable,
this woman's a witch,
a wild wonderful,
beautiful bitch.
She makes me love her,
one way or the other,
And I do whatever she wish
All for the taste of her kiss

If it wasn't for her mojo,
and black cat bone,
I could leave, girl,
and come back home.
But she ties me down
with my back to the ground,
And she rides me right down to
the bone,
Oh, Mable my freedom is gone.

When I see her dancing,
I shake with fright,
Chicken blood
and her mating rite.
The full moon surrounds her
with magic and thunder,
whenever she's holding me tight,
Oh, Mable, do I need you tonight.

Puzzle Pieces

From the beginning
Things were hard to fit
Like rough edges on a puzzle
We never were in sync.
When I laughed, you cried
Old gospel moved your feet,
While I rocked to jazz
Gentleness became you
In body and in thoughts
You moved me
and I loved it.
So we stayed even until now,
smiling....

Paradise

The eruption sloshed
the corridors of Old Main.
Truth and Beauty were done,
another week.
Friday, 4:15.
Delores and Julia
wanted to take me to Paradise.
How do you get to Paradise?
I've never been.

Take the streetcar
down Woodward to Seldon,
past the Graystone Ballroom,
Majestic Theatre,
the prison flanneled
National Bank of Detroit
and the orange painted
second-hand bookstore.

High yella Delores
with garden green eyes
reaches still higher.
Always seemed to look
for a seance to happen.
Julia wore her paradise dress
that grabbed her secure all over.

She didn't stop time when she
walked,
she just created motion
and deep froze it.
The seams of her dress
overflow just enough
to let you know what they were
holdin'.
Big gams, too.

Go to the top balcony of Para-
dise.
Lady Day looking for "Lover
Man."
"Flying Home," Hampton,
Dinah, "Ain't Nobody's Business
If I Do."

When I go back to Paradise
hear the Guarneri Quartet,
the Detroit Symphony,
I look to the top balcony.
I still hear Diz, Count, Bird,
and Mr. B's "Cottage for Sale."
You know what?
I betcha Julia is still freezin'
things.
Orchestra Hall.

Selection From "Watermelon Rinds & Cherry Pits," Broadside Press

SECTION IV — THE ENTERTAINERS

Paradise Theater Featuring Duke Ellington

Maudie Kitchen, Stage Name **Mona Desmond,** was a dancer with The Idlewild Revue. In Detroit, she also worked at places like the Flame Showbar, and El Sino. Her agents during that time were LaJune Rodgers and Rollo Vest. Today, she is a Missionary working for the Lord.
Submitted by Jeanette Vaughn

Courtesy of Virgil Rodgers Collection

Johnnie Mae Matthews

Originally born in Bessemer, AL. At age eleven, her family moved to East Orange, NJ where she played piano and sang with the church choir. Later, she met and married Artwell Matthews upon his discharge from the Army. A job with the Ford Motor Company brought them to Detroit.

In Detroit, her singing took on a whole new dimension, and Johnnie Mae sang her sultry songs throughout Paradise Valley and the Mid-west.

In 1958, she started a recording company called "Northern Records." Some of the artists she recorded were The Temptations, Mary Wells, Thelma Hopkins of "Family Affairs" who also sang with Tony Orlando & Dawn, and the famous bass player James Jamison.

Three beautiful young ladies, Rosito Sims, Beatrice Buck, and Beulah entertain **Sammy Davis**. John Hopkins is sitting on stool in rear. *Courtesy of Beatrice Buck Collection*

SPORTREE'S Lounge 1949— Several admirers gather to chat with "The Three Blazers." In front, left to right, are Charles Brown and Johnny Moore. These types of interacial gatherings were quite common in the Valley. The white gentleman standing in the light suit is Ed McKensie. In front of him, sitting in the dark shirt is Dick Jennings.

Courtesy of Beatrice Buck Collection

Paradise Lost

The swaying of the hips
As I did the shimmy
Mesmerized the patrons of the
local Barhop.
The throaty laughter
And the raunchiness of my
conversation
Made milder souls
Gawk in amazement
The confidence of my swagger
As I sashayed into the room
Was as undeniable
As the heat emanating
From the room full
Of fellow partiers.
We danced,
We laughed,
We celebrated

The 666 Dancers Mattye Gaither, Frankie Wyche, & Maybelle Moore. It's 1998 and these beautiful ladies are still dancing. *Courtesy of Beatrice Buck Collection*

Rod Rodgers Dance Company *Courtesy of Virgil Rodgers Collection*

Why?....
Because we *were.*
That's why.
It was Intoxicating,
Invigorating,
Suffocating
To be us.

As the years passed,
Our intensity — un-intensified
I no longer shimmy
Or sock-hop
But, at least,
I can still envision Paradise
Our paradise
...was not lost
It was simply
...misplaced

It will, It can,
Be discovered anew....

© 1997 Joyce Cade-Hilton

Marianne Lavan —The Body Beautiful, now living in Las Vegas, held Detroit captive during the late 1950's. *Courtesy of Virgil Rodgers Collection*

Rosalina

She spoke French fluently
As her guests arrived.
"Bonsoir monsieur, mademoiselle."
"Je m'appelle, Rosalina."
The words slipped softly
Through peppermint lips
That enjoyed the pleasure
Of an occasional kiss.
She is black as the Madonna
Whose life she does not emulate.
But her beauty cannot be hidden.
Perfume, faint as a yellow rose,
Lingers with intoxicating scents
Of Puerto Rico rum
And Irish whiskey.
She is the hostess for the evening
In a club called "Every Man's Dream."
She beams as her hips graciously
Sway to "Some Enchanted Evening".
She is tall, thin, poetically graceful
like a ballerina
Who dances like a
swan
Floating across the
pond.
Many men have seen
her,
And many want to be
seen with her,
For she is beautiful.
Like strong drink to a
weary mind,
Their worries are left
behind,
Watching as she
sashays
Across the lacquered
floor.
Their problems,
Temporarily out of
sight,
Are forgotten for one
night.
She greets her guests
With a dazzling smile.
Her name is Rosalina.

Body And Soul

Coleman Hawkins, "The Bean"
recorded "Body and Soul,"
1939 masterpiece.
My kind of jazz.
My life a wreck
you're making
Everyone waited for Body and
Soul
Time to *coote* across the floor
slower than slow,
If Gwen was there,
the studs would break
in her direction.
I only knew the two-step.
Still do.
The only dance I ever learned.
The two step
was born for Body and Soul.
No light could creep
between dancers' bodies.
I'm all for you.
To dance with Gwen
was to go places
places you had never been
places softer...
than foam on beer.

Leroy Hollis and Ruth Brown - *Courtesy of Beatrice Buck Collection*

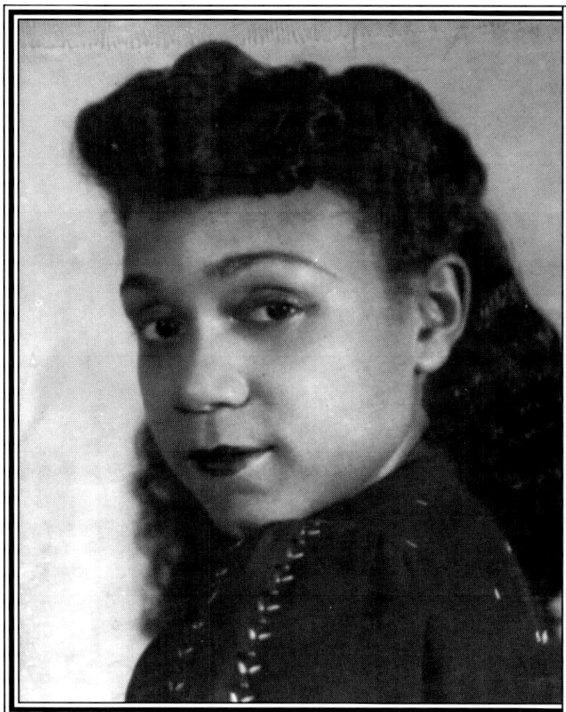

Adagio Dancers LaJune & Ernest Rodgers
Courtesy of Virgil Rodgers Collection

LaJune Rodgers

(1916-1973)
by
Debraha Watson

Mrs. LaJune Rodgers was born in Huntsville Ala bama onAugust 22, 1916, and later migrated to Detroit. She entered show business at the age of sixteen as a dancer. Years later, she and her husband Ernest Rodgers toured the country and the Caribbean as a professional Adagio team.

Upon retiring from the night-club circuit in the early fifties Ernest Rodgers established one of the city's first black Booking Agency,The Rodgers and Rodgers Theatrical Agency. After his untimely death in 1958, Mrs. Rodgers supported her five children by maintaining the Booking Agency. The agency showcased local talent and provided a sanctuary for budding musicians. Later, Mrs. Rodgers along with her sonVirgil, worked as a team to establish the "Detroit Entertainers Club," better known as the "RAPA House." The faded green painted brick house located at 96 East Fischer Freeway was a hidden gem. It housed such treasures as spicy succulent creole food, and a spiritual tea leaf reader. On any given day, the wails of a saxophone and soft stirring notes of the ancient piano drifted throughout the house.

While the RAPA House gained notoriety, Mrs. Rodgers also embarked upon other successful ventures.

In 1970, she established a writers workshop, and in 1972, her agency received a Federal Grant to fund a literary magazine, entitled"Identity" which highlighted local aspiring writers. Mrs. Rodgers' love for the Arts, business acumen, and community involvement earned her the title of "*GuardianAngel*" in the performing arts circles.

LaJune & Ernest Rodgers
Courtesy of Virgil Rodgers Collection

Mrs. Rodgers and The RAPA House

By
Calvin Robinson
(*As Told To Herbert Metoyer*)

Boy, it was really neat the way the engineers dropped that old hotel, The Detroiter, right into its basement. Too bad. Like looking at an old, old friend and saying good bye. I made a lot of money out of that hotel with my shoe shine box.

Behind the Hotel Detroiter was a school for Catholic nuns. The bishop used to come to the hotel for lunch and the cars would be double-parked on Woodward Avenue. The only other place he'd frequent was the Book Cadillac Hotel onWashington Boulevard.

A Jewish mob called *The Purple Gang* lived in the hotel mixing right in with the church people coming through. Back then, they liked their shoes shining at all times. That was a must. I liked to shine their shoes, too, because they tipped real heavy. A lot of people stayed at the Detroiter. Coming and going — day and night. The city was stepping!

On a good day, I could make almost a hundred dollars, just shining shoes. Especially on a Saturday. I would also sell newspapers through the week, making over a hundred dollars, and I was just ten years old! Unlike today, we had plenty of money. Today, the people of Detroit don't have any money or very good taste. A hip city was destroyed because most of the people, white and black, were not *cosmopolitan* enough to live in a big city that steps.

In a big city, you have to have night life. Without it, you don't have a big city. To be for real, without it, you don't have nothing. I mean, nothing. How sad.

Today, I can look across I-75 at the parking lot behind the big church on Woodward. That's where *Mrs. LaJune Rodgers' house* used to be. Close to John R., Mrs. Rodger's house was one of the largest in the city. People in the Arts often met there to socialize. Her dining room was so large that it held a small stage.

In the next block, what was once EastVernor Highway, was *Joe Louis' and Sonnie Wilson's Chicken Shack*. Across the street, was one of two black hospitals that were within four blocks of each other. The black movie theater was on the corner of Hastings and Vernor. Next door, was a big deli with the best hot dogs in the city. It also had a bar in it, so you could get a cool beer there, too.

Going north, up John R., there were a lot of little bars and a first class hotel, *The Carlton Plaza*. The Carlton had a jazz club in it called "*The Blue Note*," where all the young street players and their ladies hung out. It was a very clean and civilized place. Everyone was kind to one another. Not only were the people hip, the staff was hip. In all the years I went there, the staff always gave first class service, day or night. It was nice to just hang out there with your lady, or just drop by to have a drink. Sometimes, when you hit the door, two or three drinks would be sent to your table, arriving there before you could sit down.

Looking south of Vernor on John R., six blocks away, was the beginning of Paradise Valley. But behind Mrs. Rodgers' back door was this little club where *Art Tatum* used to play. It's still there. Across the street was the other black hospital.

Now to think about it, I really don't know how I met Mrs. Rodgers. It just seems I was always at her house. I used to live in the neighborhood, five blocks away on Beaubien near Brush, before we moved to the North End. I went to Bishop School just off of Hastings.

My neighborhood boasted a first class black Y.M.C.A. and Y.W.C.A. The Mayor used to come

LaJune Rodgers and some of the clients her Booking Agency represented. *Courtesy of Virgil Rodgers Collection*

and have lunch there almost every day. The white Y.M.C.A was four blocks away. The service from the Y's staff, in that day, you would not believe. You would eat from crystal plates and sterling silverware every meal. We also had one of the two swimming teams that were the pride of the city.

The coach's name was Buddy Wilson, and nobody in the Y.M.C.A. League, white or black, could beat Coach Wilson's team. At a time when black people were told they could not swim, we had two black swimming teams that nobody in the USA could beat, right here in the city of Detroit. I was swimming on both teams at the same time.

I started coming over to play with Virgil, Mrs. Rodgers young son. Virgil like to play. My pianist friend, Rowland Davis, and I did, too. Virgil had these two big Dobermans, *I mean big*, who seemed to have the mentality of an eleven year old human. Their discipline and training just amazed me. Everyone knows the Doberman is a hard dog to work with. But these dogs sat around the house and acted like kids.

Around this time, Mrs. Rodgers' older son, Ernie, had just gotten out of the service. He played alto saxophone, and was a cross between Hank Crosby and Cannonball Adderley. All of them had that heavy tenor sound. Like Cannon and Hank, Ernie was a natural leader and that was very important. In a good band, you can't have a raggedy leader. The band can't move with someone who can't lead. You can't get deep into the music worrying how to get out if you should step off into the hole.

With Ernie, from time to time, we'd almost drop in the hole. Then, instead of us trying to blast our way back out of the hole, Ernie would have the band change direction inside the music. As a result, we'd come out in a different way than we went in and still be cooking — driving the singer at the same time. We'd go in and out of the hole so fast, nobody could tell we ever dropped out of it.

For those of you who are unaware, Mrs. LaJune Rodgers was a Detroit In*stitution,* the matriarch of a very talented family. She and her husband made up the dance team *Rodgers and Rodgers*. When he passed away, she became a booking agent for local talent. Besides Virgil and Ernie, her other children were Rod Rodgers, *the great Alvin Ailey dancer*, and Rhonda Rodgers. It was Rhonda who helped keep everyone on their toes.

At the time I started visiting her house, Mrs. Rodgers was the booking agent for all the big name dancers of that time such as *Lottie the Body, Roxy Ann, Mona Desmond* and every good dancer in North America. Her dancers worked all over the United States and Alaska. When she wanted to expand, she started booking shows for singers, dancers, comedians, M.C.'s, and musicians. Eventually, she worked with Barry Gordy booking his acts. This was at a time when night clubs in Detroit were going six and seven nights a week. In one week, I subbed for James Jameson and worked with Hank Crosby, Joe Hunter, and Benny Benjamin. These fellas played in the band that made Motown. They were the Motown Sound.

When Barry wanted to book more shows, I got a group together. Gip Roberts was our M.C. on the mike, and Pat Pattson was our comedian. The band had a good front line — Ernie Rodgers on alto, Virgil Rodgers on trumpet, Bob Nelloms on piano, and Bobby Cruzar on drum's. I was on bass. It was deep. We were getting down playing these shows.

Soon, work picked up and we worked more and more. As

jazz clubs were fading, Barry's shows were heating up. Some of the people we worked with were Smokey and the Miracles and The Supremes. Then, Barry started recording in Joe Battles' Record Shop on Hastings and Mack Avenue. So during the daytime, while we were recording for Barry two or three times a week, we were also working six nights a week playing jazz. All the while though, the jazz scene continued to slowly close down. Jameson had me subbing for him, and Joe Hunter had Kenny Cox subbing for him.

Gradually, all of the "*cats*" started leaving one by one. That's how everyone left. One by one. It was 1959, the beginning of "*The Great Jazz Migration.*" The best jazz musicians in the world left Detroit, taking with them memories of an era when Detroit was known as the "*Jazz Capitol of the United States.*" A musician had to come here to find out how good he was. And all of the best came here to hang out. With three-thousand bars and nightclubs going day and night, they had all the work they could want. This was before Motown, when Detroit was a jazz and blues city. This was about the time I met Robin Yusef.

Robin worked with one of the shows and played guitar. One day, me and Roland went down to Mrs. Rodgers to play some with Virgil, and Robin was there. She said she was from Chicago, another place with some good players. When her show went back home, she stayed with Mrs. Rodgers and started working with some of the other shows that were coming through. When we'd come down to play with Virgil, she'd sit in with us, and we would have a good time. That sister could play that guitar!

Polly Goree, Dancer —1940's *Courtesy of Beaatrice Buck Collection*

One day, she came by my house to play some, and she had this book on positive thought. She ran it down to me, explaining how I could open up another part of my mind, not only to the music, but to more positive experiences in my life. Mrs. Rodgers was also running it down to me, so I started studying with them. This was in the late fifties, but what I learned from these ladies still carries me through life today.

Positive thought carried me through New York, the road, the west coast, and up against the best musicians in the world playing from Birdland to the Penthouse.

Shortly after my introduction to positive thought, Mrs. Rodgers started having sessions, after hours, at her house. This was the beginning of "*The RAPA House*" or the *Rodgers Academy of the Performing Arts* that quickly became center of the downtown scene. The RAPA House was no bull-shit place. I got a "gig" with Lionel Hampton's band there. Unlike now, bands came through Detroit for six nights at a time for two or three weeks. We played every night and there was no telling who would drop by. Once, Mrs. Rodgers brought John Lee Hooker in and we did a two-day recording session with him at her house.

Before long, Barry Gordy's groups were going on the road, touring for weeks at a time and work began to dry up in the city. Virgil talked about moving to Los Angeles. Roland moved to New York. Robin went on the road, then moved back to Chicago. Bob Nelloms and Bobby Cruzar were on the road with Hank Crosby and James Jameson. Joe Hunter and Benny Benjamin didn't like the road, so they stayed home. And me, well, I decided it was time for me to move to New York.

When I got to New York, I saw Jameson and the Motown show at the Apollo Theater in Harlem. We were hanging out back stage when Jameson took me outside and said, "I got something I want you to see." He took me to the touring bus and told me to look up at the top of it. That bus must've had twenty-five bullet holes in it. James said, "We got that coming through the south. I thought we were safe when we got to New York, but we ended up getting some more bullets fired on us from a cat on the show with us."

Later on, while on a brief walk, Jameson said, "You see that line of people trailing all the way down 125th Street? Well, I want you to see this cat these people go crazy over when he comes on stage. He kinda falls down, and someone comes and removes his cape. All he does is grunts and the whole house goes crazy. I mean, people get upset. And all this happens before he even begins to sing!"

Jameson told me that this was this cat's first time in New York and that he was messing up every show from the 9:00 A.M. to the 4:00 A.M., and his show still had a week to go. I asked what the cat's name was, and he said, "James Brown." This was in the fall of 1961.

Let's look at what happened to everybody. Barry and Motown became big. Ernie became band director for Northwestern High School and took the band all over the world. In the '80's, I talked with a woman musician from Chicago, who said that when Robin came back in the early '60's, she helped to open up all kind of doors for female musicians. Virgil, after living in Los Angeles for 30 years, came back to work as band director for his brother, Ernie, who had become the Principal of Northwestern.

Although Mrs. Rodgers passed away in the seventies, the RAPA House stayed open through the early '80's. Hank Crosby later wrote for Stevie Wonder and other Motown acts, and retired as an executive for a big recording company. James Jameson passed away and had a book written about him that can be purchased from the Motown Museum. Benny Benjamin also passed away. Bob Nelloms worked with Charlie Mingus' last band and still lives in New York City. Roland Davis died in New York. Bobby Cruzar worked with Motown for a long time and is retired from music.

As for me, Virgil and I still play frequently after almost thirty-one years. We resumed playing in 1995 and today it's 1998. Happy New Year!

Butterbean & Suzie *Courtesy of Richard Thomas Collection*

Courtesy of Virgil Rodgers Collection

Courtesy of Richard Thomas Collection

Billie's Demise

lady
sing no more your blues-piece
anthems
of never-ever-glad times
God-bless-the-child times
times that know
no morning kiss
lady
lady
cover your trophies
celebrating sadness
beneath buttoned sleeves
and tears
then lapse from
mournful exile
as we watch a gardenia
fall from your hair

The Beige Beauts of The Larry Steele Review "Smart Affairs"—*Courtesy of Richard Thomas Collection*

Versalle's favorite work place was the Flame Showbar - *Courtesy of Virgil Rodgers Collection*

Black Bottoms

Can you feel it
in your feet
Come on Baby
dance with me
to the Paradise beat
Jump , Baby , Jump ...
Swing—to the Black Bottom
Bump
Jitter your bug—Stomp
Hulley your Gulley, Ba-a-a-a-by
Ho-o-o-ld me tight, Baby,
From now
Through Saturday night

New Ocella Hotel
Southwest corner Catherine & Hastings Sts.
Finest Hotel for colored people in the west now opened. Rates $2.50 and up. Special weekly rates. Steam heat, hot & cold water in each room. Bath house in connection, for ladies and gentlemen,
Showers, needle and tub baths
HORACE F. CANNON, Manager

SUNNIE WILSON'S
ROLLER RINK
★
Special Attention

★

SUNNIE WILSON'S
Bowl - O - Drome
★
26 - ALLEYS - 26

SUNNIE WILSON'S
Mark Twain Hotel
★
52 GARFIELD
TE. 1-8260

Detroit's Finest and Most Ideally Located Hotel

★

SUNNIE WILSON'S
Cocktail Lounge

710 East Forest
TErrace 2-9106

Longest Bar in the World

Virgil Rodgers —*Courtesy of Virgil Rodgers Collection*

Virgil Rodgers

by

Heather Buchanan

A great jazzman on the Detroit music scene, Virgil Rodgers had an early introduction to the entertainment world. Born to Ernest and LaJune Rodgers, Adagio Dancers who entertained audiences throughout the United States and Cuba, Virgil joined the family act as a tap dancer and acrobat with his brothers. The Rodgers family eventually settled in Detroit to open a theatrical booking agency. By the age of sixteen, Virgil was performing professionally on the trumpet at various clubs in Detroit, Saginaw, Flint and Toledo, Ohio.

After high school, Virgil played trumpet with the United States Air Force Band, touring North Africa, and performing in various jazz clubs from Casablanca to Robat, Morocco. Afterwards, he returned to Detroit to perform with the Jimmy Wilkins Big Band and Motown Recording Studio. He also played drums and percussion with the Larry Steele Review and Maurice King's Band at the Flame Showbar, backing some of the top entertainers in the country.

Marlene Rodgers

Virgil later worked as a theatrical booking agent with his mother LaJune, and together they formed the Detroit Entertainer's Club, which later became known as the RAPA House (*Rodgers Academy for The Performing Arts*).

Virgil then journeyed to Los Angeles, California, where he worked at various recording studios and clubs with artists such as Tommy Flanagan, George Bletso, Papa John Grech (violin) and Roger Spotts Big Band. While in L.A., Virgil earned a B.A. degree in Music and a Masters Degree in Multi-cultural Education from the University of Los Angeles, CA. Virgil then took his talents into the class room, teaching jazz at Crenshaw High School, later reputed to be one of the best high school jazz bands in L.A..

Virgil also opened a "RAPA House West" in Los Angeles with his wife, Marlene. The RAPA House West soon became a west coast mecca for musicians across the country.

Thirty years later, Virgil returned to Detroit to fill the position of Director of Northwestern High School's Jazz Ensemble, where he has taught for the past four years. Virgil is presently forming a new music program at Hampton Middle School. Virgil has also formed his own jazz group, Visions.

Don't know what Gina is doing these days. Pinky still lives & works in Detroit. People used to line up at the door to see the Amazing Caldonia, a 65 year old contortionist. Virgil Rodgers was an all around Detroit Musician (singer, percussionist, & trumpet player).

Courtesy of Virgil Rodgers Collection

PITTSBURGH COURIER

Rita Graham, Vocalist, worked Flame Showbar with Benny Jones Band -*Courtesy of Virgil Rodgers Collection*

Romy Rand, a Nancy Wilson Type Singer
Courtesy of Virgil Rodgers Collection

Harry Belafonte - *Courtesy of Richard Thomas* Collection

Line of People waiting to get into The El Sino - *Courtesy of Richard Thomas Collection*

Sarah Vaughn

Sassy Sarah, Sassy Sarah.
Mellow voice, like a bird in
flight.
And between the sheets,
my lover comes.
Sassy Sarah, Sassy Sarah
Stirring hearts & souls
With your chords of gold
Making rhythm outward/inward
Untold

Sassy Sarah, Sassy Sarah
Singing —shifting darkness
Into light and rest into
Peace.
Sassy Sarah, Sassy Sarah
Who will sing those melodies
Of sunsets & stars in the sky.
Causing us to reflect &
Regret

Sassy Sarah, Sassy Sarah
Death's joy and our sorrow
Who will fill your be-bop,
hip-hop shoes.

Yeah, yeah, yeah,
Yeah, yeah,
Yeah....

Kline's Show Bar

(For Jessie & Annie Ruth)

It ain't nothing but a night out
a chance to break day
with eggs smothered in grease
and curse every bird I see
It ain't nothing but wishing
I could sleep with
all them jazz solos
cause they get so close some-
times

It ain't nothing but a night out
a sham like these rhinestones
but something I picked out
and wanna keep
like Jessie calling me
"Dollin" at the door
and Annie Ruth
fixing me a drink

Selection from "Sorrow's End," Broad-side Press

The El Sino Band - *Courtesy of Richard Thomas Collection*

Torchy, 666 Club Shake Dancer & Carmen Lauchie-Bradley having lunch, 1946 - *Submitted by Reginald Gibbs*

Ernie Rodgers & His Band at the "Black Velvet."
Courtesy of Virgil Rodgers Collection

Title for Doctoral Dissertation

The political
ramifications
of jazz
as it affects
the id
of black male musicians
in the context
that it affords black males
the only avenue
of self expression
on which they can walk
and encounter
few interruptions
and very little,
if any,
bullshit....

Selection from "Sorrow's End," Broadside Press

Sunset Theory

(Who said the world is round?)

In dragnets of color
The sun creeps toward the
edge
A cross-breed of reds
A mulatto in orange
A finger painting
too wet to continue

It shifts again
Making a last display
Then trips and falls
Into the garden of some
Sleepy Chinese boy
Skirting Yangtze and pagoda
Proclaiming a new day

Selection from "Sorrow's End," Broadside Press

Urge For Home

The farmer lays aside,
his old rusty plow
Wipes his calloused hand,
across his sweaty brow.
Evening shadows yawn,
and stretch out their manes.
Swallow birds turn,
to nest again.

Shrimp boats heading steady,
for the distant shore,
Porpoise all in trail,
turn out to sea once more.
Sea gulls settle gracefully
down upon the sand
The cooing turtle doves
bring peace across the land.

The sun sets hard,
upon the desert plains
The eagle takes her young
beneath her tender wing
Buzzards circle high,
scratching the purple sky
The coyote fills the night
with its mournful cry

The work whistle echoes
from the lumber mill
And ends the day again,
for the spinning wheel
Crickets tune-up solo
to sing their symphony

Lt. Herbert Metoyer— Naples, Italy, 1958, Enroute from Tripoli, Libya to Amsterdam, Holland. A long flight for an L-19 Aircraft.

Capt. Herbert Metoyer (*Special Forces*) with His Mother, Ruby; Father, Herbert, Sr.; and Brother, Manley. 1962, three months prior to shipping out to Vietnam.

SECTION V – MILITARY/SPORTS

The distant guns
on the battlefield
seem to be mocking me

And so, I think of Ruby
and how far away I've roamed
As the evening sun sets
I get the urge
to lay aside my guns
and head for home....

© 1986 Herbert R. Metoyer
To my Mother, Ruby Lee, from Vietnam, 1963

Two Colored Coast Guard Sailors Eugene Kelly & Robert Williams who spent most of their duty as cooks for white officers & sailors — the only jobs given to Negroes. *Submitted by Geraldine Metoyer*

Beg A Coin

I have been husband,
father, john to whore,
My country's mighty
sword arm in the war,
Swam bare feet off Oriental shore.
Flame-throwers ignited
my poor core
When I saw results along
the streets of Saigon —
cripples raising what's left of hands.
I wondered, do they curse
their own heartbeats,
While warmongers invade
their holy lands
Imagine how a tank would look to you
Before it piece-mealed you
with chattering guns.
Would you wonder—
What else can I do,
But try to beg a coin
from murder's sons?"
I cry— "How can they live
with burns for art?"
While I try to raise
what's left of heart.

In Korea, they were friends— buddies, inseparable. But, back home, well.... *Submitted by Geraldine Metoyer*

Anxious to serve his country, Inkster Realtor, **Willie C. Williams,** put his age up and joined the Air Force in 1943 at age 14. He served as an Aircraft Weapons Repairman.
Submitted by Karen Williams

The Battle of Tam Hut

We were called into Tam Hut
On January Two
We would never have gone
If we'd only knew
We were supporting the ARVAN
A Group without guts
Attacking a village
Of straw covered huts.

A ten copter mission
A hundred troop load
Three lifts are now over
A fourth on the road
The VC start shooting
They fire a big blast
We off-load the ARVAN
They sit on their ass.

One copter is crippled
Another sits down
Attempting a rescue
There's two on the ground.
A Huey returns now
To give them some aid
The VC so accurate
They shoot off a blade.
Four pilots are wounded
Two crewmen are dead
And when its all over
A good day for the Reds.
Our boys lay in the paddies
All covered with slime
One hell of a sun bath
Eight hours at a time.

An Armored Battalion
Stayed hid in a trance
One US Captain died trying
To make them advance.
The paratroopers landed
A magnificent sight
There was hand to hand combat
And not a VC in sight.

When the News was reported
The ARVAN had won
But the VC's were laughing
Over their captured guns.
The newsmen were trying
To get some true words
But the news as reported
Was all for the birds.

So, all you pilots take warning
When tree lines are near
Let's land those Dam Copters
One mile to the rear....

© 1963 CW4 Pappy Wright, A Battlefield Poet

This poem was written about a true battle that occurred in Vietnam, January 2, 1963. This battle was a good example of the unwillingness of the ARVAN (South Vietnamese) to fight. Many times, after we would off-load the ARVAN in the Landing Zone, instead of firing on the VC (Viet Cong), they would shoot at us as we lifted off. This was documented several times.
Very little of the news that appeared in the newspapers during that time was factual or accurate. Every thing was designed to make the progress of the war appear successful, when things, in reality, were in chaos.
Pappy wrote this song immediately after the battle. That night, when we gathered to honor our dead, we sung it to the tune of "On Top of Old Smokey," while getting plastered on Vietnamese Beer in our Lean-To Cabana Officers Club in Nha Trang, Vietnam.
Herbert R. Metoyer, Major, US Army, Retired.

Repent

When final trumpet
resounds
o'er lands and seas,
Then even holy men
resume their knees,
While all the sinners,
though too late,
repent
The lives they wasted,
with their knees unbent.
Too late for the
Rose of Sharon's bud,
When Armageddon
washes us in blood
That will not save,
though Christ already gave
His own, that we might
never fear the grave.
So gather, friends,
wherever you may choose,
To share your every sin,
or share Good News.
Be careful, though,
to choose the proper place,
Remembering, one day,
you'll see God's face,
And if you want to hear
Him say, "Well done!"
Take up your cross,
and lay aside your gun.

© 1997 Marc Maurus

1/lt. Herbert & Geraldine Metoyer in Rome, Italy for Olympics, 1960

George Moore Above. His Unit's picture is below.
Submitted by Peggy A. Moore

Our Flag

A symbol of our unity,
Of common bonds, and dignity,
A cloth of hope, and Freedom
Rings,
For every human being.

Reminder of the strength
within,
Of kinship, home and loyal
friends,
Reminder that so many care,
For every human being.

On land, at sea, or in the air,
In wind, and storm, and
sunlight's glare,
The Flag waves high and mighty
there,
For every human being.

The Flag waves for humanity,
For faith, and hope, and charity,
A symbol of our pride, our
peace,
Our harmony... Our Flag.

Two World War Two Soldier Boys - *Submitted by Peggy A. Moore*

Clarence Williams — Korea 1953. War is Hell.
Submitted by Geraldine Metoyer

Wish Upon A Scar

Now I know why love
must needs be blind,
Not everyone worth loving
is a star.
In fact, a mark of living
is a scar,
It shows no fear to seek out,
or to find.
I'd rather flirt with beauty
of the mind,
Learning that has traveled
near and far,
From sanctuary to
the local bar,
Withstood a beating
trying to be kind.
Swiftly, let our mental
selves embrace,
Before life turns to shuffle
off the coil.
Amidst the lightning,
upturn grinning face,
Only true friends grant
a heartbeat's boil.
Yearn to look beyond
the mirror's trace,
To love, and love again,
before we're soil

© 1997 Marc Maurus

Passing Judgement

Let my content be the judge
Not the robe
For like prose
I must be read in order to know.
Wrapped in cloth,
The foundation of my essence
My complexion deceives.
Gainful insights
To my attributes
To my soul.
Judge me by my composition,
Judge me whole.

© 1998 Sylvia McClain

Lt. Alexander Jefferson, Tuskegee Airman, P-51 Mustang Escort Pilot.

Lt. Colonel Alexander Jefferson
US Air Force, Retired

The Encounter

(A True Story)
By
Alexander Jefferson

It was a warm sunny day on the twelfth of August, 1943, when I, Lieutenant Jefferson, a member of the 332nd Fighter Group, climbed aboard my Red-tailed P-51 Mustang and soared into the wild blue yonder to attack German Radar Stations along the coast of France. On one of my strafing passes, at fifty feet above the ground, I flew right into a hail of 20mm shells. There was a loud explosion and immediately the cockpit filled with hot oil and smoke. Realizing that I was on fire and too low to bail out, I horsed back on the stick and used my remaining airspeed to gain as much altitude as possible. When I reached approximately eight-hundred feet, my aircraft shuddered violently, stalled, then rolled onto its back. At that point, I took a deep breath and ejected, snatching my rip cord the moment I was clear. Helplessly, I watched as my aircraft, my steed, my ride back home, crashed in flames into an open field. With a silent prayer, I tightened my grip on my risers and

waited with abated breath as I drifted into the waiting arms of a very angry German patrol. As I tumbled to the ground, they rushed toward me with bayonets drawn and I feared the worse until they suddenly realized that I was black—probably the first they had ever seen from the look on their faces. I suppose it was this fact that made them back down and spare my life.
Instead, I quickly became a prized oddity, something to look at and jabber about.

They took me, then, at gun point to a villa about twenty miles east of Toulon where I was told to sit on the verandah beside a wrought iron table no more than a hundred feet from the water's edge. So I sat, looking out across the azure blue waters of the Mediterranean, wondering about my uncertain future and what would be said once my family and friends found out that I was missing.

Some moments later, a German officer strolled out onto the porch, looked at me coldly, then lit a cigarette.

"What is your name?" he asked in perfect English.

"Alexander Jefferson, First Lieutenant, US Army Air Corps, Serial Num..."

"Let's forget the formalities for the moment, Lieutenant. Where in the States are you from? Have you ever been to Washington?"

"No excuse, sir," I replied immediately in *boot camp* fashion as a way of avoiding having to answer his questions.

"I only ask," the officer continued, "because I went to school in your country. I went to the University of Michigan. Do you know of it?"

"I know of it," I replied hesitantly. But deep down inside, I wanted to tell this representative of the Master Race that I was a graduate of Clark University in Atlanta with a Master's from Howard University in Washington, D.C..

"Good. Have you ever been to Michigan? It is a wonderful state."

"I'm from Michigan, Detroit."

At the mention of Detroit, the German Officer's demeanor changed completely. For the next thirty minutes, I sat listening as the officer excitedly told me about his adventures into "Paradise Valley," about the fun he had while there drinking, carousing, and fraternizing with the local girls, mentioning several by name — none of which I knew. He also rattled off the names of most of the night spots and hotels in the Valley, especially the "Three Sixes" which he stated was his favorite.

"... Yes some of the best times in my life were spent in Detroit's Valley. Let's hope this war ends soon so we can get back to the things that really matter," he said when he was done.

With that, he offered me one of his cigarettes (which I accepted), shook my hand, then stood on the porch in a typical Nazi stance, watching silently and forlornly as they loaded me aboard a truck to be transported to a POW Camp in the interior.

It really is a small world, I thought to myself as the beach and the quaint villa faded off into the distance. At first, my feelings had been a little raw, hearing him speak about the "*Good*" loving he received from our black girls back home. In the end, however, I was truly thankful for their efforts in behalf of the war. Truly thankful, indeed....

Lt. Jefferson sat out the remainder of the war until he was liberated. An excellent artist, he recorded his whole adventure in pen and crayon drawings that he hopes to publish soon. The drawings on the opposite page are samples of his work — the editor.

Inkster Realtor, Willie C. Williams at height of his professional boxing career in 1950's.

June 26, 1948, Mamie Montgomery and friends attend Joe Louis/Walcott fight in New York. Also in picture is Thurston McKinney —*Submitted by Mamie Montgomery*

Louisiana Fite Nite

Everyone up with the sun
MaDear singing "Deep River"
Daddy gone to the mill
Peddler in the street
Singing his 3-note selling song
Wagon loaded with sweet
potatoes, milk, peanuts
watermelons, cantaloupes,
greens, fruit, hogshead cheese
and Hadacol
No washing today
MaDear baking 'taters and Jelly
cakes
Roasting peanuts and soaking sun
tea
My job to pick a big ole jar of
Honeysuckles
For the top of our RCA radio

Mid-day,
Hot, air still,
Nothing moving 'cept the clouds
and a few Dragon Flies
Dog under the house sleeping
Me, too

Evening come
Everybody up, stirring around
listening for the sawmill
Time-to-Quit-Work whistle
Trying to get friends
With somebody what gots a radio
Joe Edwards sittin'
Under his 'simmon tree
Whuping on his steel box guitar.
Makes it talk while
He sings the blues

Sun down, dust falls, time to play
Us boys play Dodge Ball
Girls play "Catch Lightning Bugs
Put 'em in a Jar."
Dookie rubbing up against
Stella Jean's titties
Trying to coax her in the bushes.
She went?
Old folks sitting on their garrets
In the cool
Telling lies, fanning mosquito flies
Somebody checks the clock
Shouts, "'Bout dat Time."
Everybody anxious
Run inside and get a place to seat
The "Shadow" going off.
The "Fight" coming on.
Lilly Mae come
MaDear say she don't lye no liquor
in her house
Lilly Mae say she don't mind
Her drunk 'fore she gits there
Got on a short skirt

— Joe Louis —
Courtesy of Richard Thomas Collection

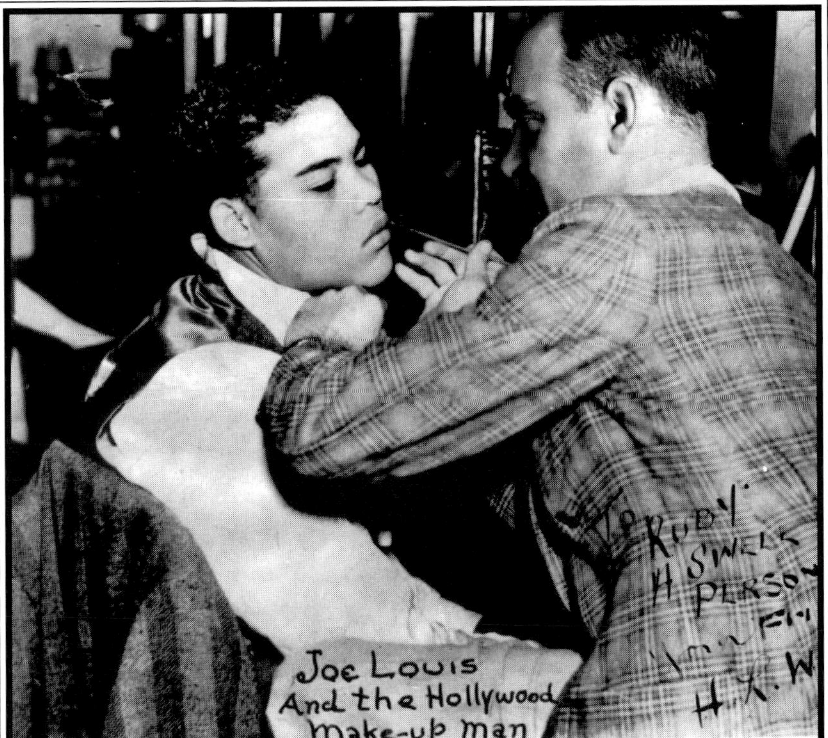

Courtesy of Richard Thomas Collection

Don't care how she sits, too
My seat —
On the flo' directly in front
End of every round
Lilly Mae jumps up
Do's her Coochie-Coo dance.
Sinful
MaDear checks
To see if Daddy *ain't* watching
He is
She cuts him some eyes

She don't like no mess like that
Corn bread, he agitated
Stomps his feet on the floor
Keeps on slapping Daddy 'cross
the back, hard
Daddy getting mad
He wants to get up and
Put one across Cornbread's lips
I know, I can tell
But... he don't

Fight over. Joe Louis wins
Wins for the entire Negro race
My Idol,
Still Champion of the
Whole Wide World
Everybody on their feet
Whooping and hollering
Everybody proud
Cause white-folks think
Joe Louis something special
Maybe, someday thcy'll
Think we're special, too
Somebody bumps the radio
Knocks over the honeysuckles
The jar hits the flo'
Cornbread says, "O," "Oh..."
Daddy says, "Dammit to hell.
That's enough."
Makes them all go home
Me, I'm sick
Five 'tatoes and
Three bags of peanuts
Don't set too well
I need to go do-do
But the outhouse is out aways
Besides, its dark out there
Got griffins and snakes out
there, too
I hurry, jump in bed
Nightmare time
Lilly Mae and them hot thighs
what's on my mind....

© 1998 Herbert R. Metoyer

Courtesy of Richard Thomas Collection

Unknown Colored Soldier Boy, WWII - *Courtesy of Jacqueline Caffey Collection*

Champion Track Team 1927 — *Courtesy of the Orlin Jones Collection*

Baseball -
Submitted by Minnie Brogdon

Baseball — *Submitted by Peggy A. Moore*

Women's Gym Class, Central Community Center, Detroit, 1931
Courtesy of Orlin Jones Collection

Wrong Place

Death round here is
nothing new to them.
She lost her brother
when she was only ten.

Shot right there
before her very own eyes,
Screams and shots were heard
as he laid there to die.

Why he got shot?
A big question
round here

Simply cause he was
in the wrong place
at the wrong time

on this certain
day of the year!

© 1997 Michanda Lynne Gant (Age 14)

Ramblings

Ramblings of a spidery hand,
across an empty page.
So much wisdom,
pain and anger,
for someone so young in age.
But feel he must,
the malice and mistrust,
from the shards of
his broken dreams.
Though they cut him at night,
when his mind takes flight.
He still holds it together
at the seams.
And while the sands of time
still flow like wine,
pain and memories
don't fade away.
So he raises his head
and smiles instead,
through the tears
of another day....

© 1996 V. duwon Jackson

SECTION VI — THE STRUGGLE

The Sky Is Crying

If a light does shine
inside of me,
It's one I just can't see
All I see are the creeping
shadows of my own
pain and misery

I feel comfortable
as I sit here in the dark
I'd much rather
be here alone
The thunder claps,
the lightning flash
reminding me of a place
I once called home.

Just outside
my tiny cell window
The Heavens begin to part
A drop hits my eye,
rolls down my cheek,
and vanishes
into the dark

© 1996 V. duwon Jackson

Courtesy of Orlin Jones Collection

Courtesy of Orlin Jones Collection

Burton Historical Library

DETROIT PEOPLES NEWS

The 1943 Riot

by

Debraha Watson

On Sunday, June 20, 1943 Detroit became an urban battlefield — littered with debris and broken glass. Blood stained streets and charred ruins cast dark shadows from Hastings Street to Gratiot and Ferry Avenues. There are varying accounts as to what caused the critical state of affairs. Some reported that it occurred as a result of an altercation between a Negro and a White man on Belle Isle during a humid Sunday afternoon. Others' state that twin false rumors, exacerbated an already tense racial climate.

Unidentified whites started a rumor that a white woman had been raped and killed by Negroes on the Belle Isle Bridge. Another rumor was started by Leo Tipton, a black man, who allegedly instigated the race riot. Reports state that Mr.Tipton dashed into a club patronized by Negroes and announced over the loudspeaker microphone that a "colored" woman and her baby had been killed by a mob of whites. Five hundred revelers responded by rushing to Belle Isle to "Take care of the whites."

To add fuel to an already raging fire, on the evening of June 21, 1943 Moses Kiska, a 58 year old Negro was shot through the heart, while waiting on a street car at Mack Avenue and Chene. Three white youths, Aldo Traini 16, Armendo Mastantuano 20, and Robert Cattone 17 confessed to the racially motivated murder. Accounts state that they took this man's life because they had a rifle and wanted to have some fun "shooting niggers." A fourth man Anthony Saraceno was implicated (the weapon was found in his car), but he never confessed.

The racial climate had been smoldering openly for more than a year following a confrontation between Blacks and whites over which race was going to occupy the Sojourner Truth housing projects. The blacks who had been deprived of public housing wanted it because they had been confined to a small deteriorating part of the city. The whites wanted it to keep the city white and the Negroes in their place, and they wanted it despite the fact that it was named for a Black female freedom fighter.

Finally, in the summer of 1943, the violence erupted and the valley became a war zone. Stores were smashed and looted. Cars and residences were set afire. Some Negro store owners escaped the destructive reign by marking the words "colored" on their property. The city officials held a series of meetings as conditions deteriorated. Finally, they declared a "modified martial law," which imposed a curfew from 10:00 P.M. until 6:00 A.M.. They also placed a ban on alcohol. It was only after a tour of the riot torn city by Mayor Ed Jefferies that the situation was declared out of control. Governor Kelly, then, formally requested Federal troops from President Roosevelt.

On June 22, 1943, thousands of Federal troops were called in to quell the riots. General William Guthner of Chicago was in command, and an operation base was set up in Grand Circus Park. It was reported that alarms rang throughout the night, and armored cars and army trucks patrolled the streets in an effort to restore law and order. Records indicate that there were several incidents of sniper attacks in the area of Hastings and Madison. Soldiers responded by firing more than 200 rounds of ammunition and throwing tear gas bombs. Several people were injured in this melee. All total twenty-five Negroes and nine whites were killed. Some of the cases remain unsolved.

The aftermath of the riot left many unanswered questions and accusations. Some Black leaders such as Arthur Bowman, Chairman of the Negro Youth Council for Victory and Democracy thought that the Klu Klux Klan (KKK) was responsible for the riot. A "formal" investigation determined that they were not. On another note, a Recorders Court psychiatrist (Dr. Selling) was reported to have examined thousand of rioters in detention to determine their "psychological and environmental characteristics." He theorized that ignorance, and in some cases, substandard mental equipment was the underlying factor in their destructive behavior. It was also believed that persons, both black and white, who engaged in riotous acts were not social human beings.

The Recorders Court was weighted down by these "anti-so-

Burton Historical Library

Burton Historical Library

cial" human beings. By all accounts stiff penalties were handed out to both Negro and white rioters. There remains, however, some question as to the fairness and availability of legal counsel to the Negroes charged, for the courts appear to have been an active obstacle that prevented Negroes from obtaining a fair trial. One legal giant, Elvin L. Davenport, President of the Wolverine Bar Association offered the services of the association's legal brigade of seventy-five attorneys. The Judge (Scallen) initially refused. Negro community leaders remained relentless and finally, Judge Scallen allowed the attorneys to counsel the detained, but only — if the lawyers knew the individuals by name. The Negroes they didn't know, well... that's another story. Isn't it?

The situation remained tense in the city for several months, but eventually the city began to heal.

Approximately a month after the riot began an interracial committee headed by Reverend T. T. Bumbraugh, secretary of the Detroit Council of Churches, and Reverend Charles A. Hill, pastor of Hartford Avenue Baptist church initiated the back to work movement. Public Aid was also provided for those whose lives had been severely altered by the riot. Detroiters slowly and painfully took steps to restore a sense of normalcy back to their community.

———

Courtesy of Orlin Jones Collection

Hasting Street —*Burton Historical Library*

Shadow Boxer

If the eyes are truly
the windows to the soul,
Then where are the doors?
The *back* one in particular
I'm asking because I believe
mine is hanging open.
For my soul has
abandoned me.
When I stare into the mirror,
I feel as if I'm looking
into an empty house.
I'm told that one's
conscience is his soul's voice
A conscience...?
Well that's another thing
that seems to be amiss
Not that I can blame him
for leaving the way he did
We fought one another
for twenty years
He always wanted me
to do right
And for some reason
I can't explain,
I was determined
to do wrong.
They say you don't miss
a good thing until it's gone.
Well, I don't want to fight
myself anymore,
I'm tired,
This fast life ain't everything
they said it was.
I definitely need that
voice of reason.
Help me, before I
destroy myself.
I don't want to die.
If you know of a way.....

© 1996 V. duwon Jackson

A Window With A View

I toss, I turn, I wake,
and I think in the solitude
Trying to hold on
to my slippery sanity
My metaphor for life.
I toss, I turn, I wake,
and I think in the night
Staring at the silence
that lays just outside
the commotion of my mind
What has brought me
to be the way that I am?
What brings me to
moments like this?
I toss, I turn, I wake,
and I remember
I used to have a family,
I used to have freedom,
I used to have a future,
I used to have love
I used to have...
I used to have....
I toss, I turn, I wake,
and I grieve,
For I have no family,
no freedom,
no future,
only time
Just time.. time...
time....

I toss, I turn, I wake,
and I look
Through the grill, the screen,
and beyond the glass;
Past the razor-wire fence,
the tower of the guards,
Out across the night
and the dusty cotton fields,
Suddenly, I smile
I have a window...
with a view.

© V. duwon Jackson 1996

V. duwon Jackson— Was convicted for Assault with a Deadly Weapon at the *age of eighteen*. He is now incarcerated in Abilene, TX. His new aspirations are to become a poet and mystery writer. He contacted the Guild and asked for our help. We believe he has outstanding potential — don't you? Let's hope he stays on track.
Submitted by Mildred Jackson

Sad Woman

I often find myself alone,
because of the things I do or say.
Everyone who's ever tried
to come close,
I managed to push away.
Don't know why
I've made it so hard.
Lost in life, I sought a
place to hide.
For eighteen years,
I gave you Hell.
Still you stood with me,
by my side.
My Sad Woman,
I've always made you cry.
But through your tears,
you saw something
good and true.
Now when I start to wonder
if anyone cares
I know without a doubt,
you... do.

Mirror

I'm not afraid to ponder
puzzles, traps,
Or tinker with the
mysteries of life,
The crossword jigsaws
of our fences, gaps,
How little ones move
from me through my wife.
I've soldiered 'cross
the sullen battlefields,
Witnessing men's
cruelty to men,
Agog at all the ways
the weapon wields,
Breaks against serenity of Zen.
I've wept with angels,
singing tears of strife,
Compared them to the blood
of pandered past.
Where find the answers
for this wayward life,
Where make the change,
in playwright or in cast?
I choose today to neither
yield nor brood,
For it's enough for me
to be not food.
Since sweet tyrannosaur
got in the mood,
And Christian, eaten,
by the Roman booed,
Or pygmies darted,
blowgunned, sewing lips,
Shrunk heads,
ate missionaries from the vat,
I've wondered, do these
monsters plunge their hips,
Lift their breasts
to suckle baby fat,
Or cheer the blitzkrieg,
throwing wide the door
To grinding tread
across an upturned face,
For pocket money
beat to death the whore,
Use the blood
to boost to outer space,
Never walking through
the door within
To face Chernobyl
with uneasy smile.
We humans (hah!) shrug,
shed our molten sin,
And Sisyphus up
one more hungry mile.

Black Love

This is a black poem.
The sound is black.
The narrator is black.
This poem is black soul.
If you are pretending black,
this poem ain't you.
But if you have neck bone spirit,
catfish marrow;
collard greens,
'taters,
clabber milk,
green onions,
fat back,
grits/hoe cakes/
snap beans and rice back bone,
this poem is you.

If you ever stood
in a number three tin tub,
watching grease rise
white hate,
this poem is you.

This poem is strong.
Black Bottom and
Sugar Hill strong.
Black love breathes on this
poem.
It was baptized black misery.
Hung out on rugged place,
crossed the Mason Dixon Line
singing "We Shall Overcome."
This poem talks
Rats, roaches,
cotton mills,
cutting cane/plowing acres/
pulling corn/picking cotton
and working boss Charlie's farm
to get deeper in debt.

It is heartache, pain,
separation and degradation.
This poem is you.

The bones of this poem
are black.
The blood, spirit
thoughts and aspirations
are black.
This poem oozes black.
Explodes black.
This poem is Martin,
Malcolm,
Emmett Till and
Medgar Evers black.
It eulogizes warriors
who paid the price
for us to be black.

This poem is you.

Night Riders

Hey, what y'all doing knocking
on m'door dis time of night?
And why y'all dressed up
in dem sheets like dat?
Som'thing wrong?
No, Suh, I can't read.
No, Suh, I wouldn't lie to you.
Watch it, Suh. You almost
hit me with dat gun butt.
No, suh. I ain't lying, too.
I found dat ragedy old
bible-book laying side de road.
I keeps it to press out
4-leaf clovers.
Sells 'em to folks for
good luck. Dat's all.
I can't read one word
and my chillin' can't neither.
Is dat you Mr. Perry?
What y'all want here, Suh?
I ain't don' nuthin' wrong.
Jes minding my own business
like I always don'.
Wait a minute, Suh, don't
drag me out de house.
My missus is doing po'ly.
'Specting to drap dat baby
any day now.
Mr. Perry, I know dat's you
and yo' two boys out ther'.
Dis here, is me, ole Shine.
Why y'all let'um treat me like
dis.
Please Suh, I ain't no hog.
It ain't right to go tying
up no man like dis.
Mr. Perry, say somthin' t'um.
My momma is the one
what raised up dem two
fine boys of your'n.
I helped, too.
Took 'em fishing
when dey was old 'nough.
Taught 'em how to make dey
first Nigga Shooters.
Please, Suh, make 'em
turn me loose.
C'mon, Suh, leave my
breeches on.
Don't take 'em off.
Dat's shameful,
what you doing,Suh.
Oooouu-Wee. Ohh Lordy,
Lordy! Dat cigar hurts.
Please, Suh, don't burn me
down dair no mo'.!
Burn me somewhere else!
Oh Lord, Mr. Perry!
If you got one once of goodness
in you, help me, please.
Tell 'em I's a good nigga.
You knows I is.
No, Suh, I don't want to get
up in back of Mr. Patti's truck.
Git away. Leeve me 'lone.
Y'all know Mr. Patti don't lye
no nigga's to touch his truck.
Dis here is too high up.
Put me back on the ground, Suh.
Old Shine, here, ain't gon'
be no worry to y'all.
Oh Lord, Bessie! Bessie!
If you hears me, gal,
run somewhere and hide.
Mr. Perry helping 'em put
the rope round my neck.
Bessie, if you hears me,
you too close. Run, gal. Run.
Lord, God in Heben,
dis ain't right.
Get up and look down here
behind you.
Des white folks doing
some bad behavior.
Lord, please come down here
and stop dis mess.
I know you don't have a lot of
time to waste on Black folks,
But we's your chillun, too, Lord.
Ain't we?
For once, don't turn yo' back.
I know I ain't been perfect,
but I tries.
Lord, if you coming, hurry.
Come quick.
Somebody moving the truck.
And Lord, If you don't make it,
I's sorry I told dem
white folks dat lie.
I's sorry, Lord. I knows how.
I knows how to rea....

Foolish Dreams

I was walking down the street,
When I saw this old black man.
Sitting beside the bar room door.
With a bottle in his hand.
He looked at me with a twinkle,
Said, "Son you sure look fine,
Dressed up in that suit of clothes,
And wearing your college mind."
He said, "You know, there ain't
much difference,
Between you and me.
Born and raised in a different time,
Still neither one is free."

Well, I stood there amazed,
So I told that old fool,
I was, me, a college graduate,
And he'd never been to school.
He said, "Son don't get excited,
It's a twix and in between,
If you know who controls the
money,
Then you knows what I mean."

He said, "How long were they fly-
ing,
Them rockets up to that moon.
Before they let a black man,
Taste from the glory spoon.
He said, "You know —
I once was a young man
With dreams just like you,
I'd climb up and they'd kick me
down,
Wasn't nothing I could do.

CHORUS:
Then he told me about the good
times,
The best that he had seen,
About the steam locomotive,
The lighter than air machine.
Then he told me about the bad
times,
The worst that he had seen,
About the Big War across the wa-
ter,
And all his foolish
dreams.
Then he was gone
Then he was gone...
gone.. gone.
Like the very last note
Of a sad, sad song.

So I did look around,
Everything he said was
true,
It was all the same from
any side,
And from any point of
view.
As I closed his eyes,
And crossed his hands,
Suddenly, I realized
He was a kind, gentle
man.
Fare-the-well, my old
friend,
What a good friend you
have been,
I see now our destiny,
Is still blowing in the
wind.
So, I walked away,
My head hanging down,
Got so mad, I took my Cap and
Gown,
And threw them on the ground.

CHORUS:
Yes, he told me about the good
times,
The best that he had seen,
About the steam locomotive,
The lighter than air machine.
Then he told me about the bad
times,
The worst that he had seen,
About the Big War across the wa-
ter,
And all his foolish dreams.
Then I was gone,
Then I was gone... gone.. gone.
Like the very last note
Of a sad, sad song....

Written to commemorate the 1st space flight of a Black Astronaut.

Submitted by Minnie Brogdon

Officer Henderson "Ben" Turpin

Ben Turpin

Law Man from Paradise

By Cheryl Wells

Often times, folklore derived from black history is riddled with paradoxical figures who represent a particular spectrum of history during hard times and demographic shifts. They capture the imagination through their accomplishments or because of their notoriety. In this respect, we can consider Henderson "Ben" Turpin to be one of the defining legendary stories of our time. His story is the emergence of a black male power image in a white dominated society.

By the time Ben Turpin was appointed a police officer on August 1, 1927 and assigned to the Third Precinct on Gratiot Avenue, forty (40) other Negro officers had preceded him. Although police records document this fact, no one in the community seems to recall the names of these officers, and some Black Bottom, Paradise Valley residents would argue that they never existed. Or if there were other Black officers, maybe they were hidden away doing insignificant tasks. They certainly were not out in the field harassing white citizens.

Turpin, however, was visible. At times, he appeared to be a shrewd, cynical outsider given to languid moments of philanthropy and sudden violence. No one remembers that Ben Turpin was a shoeshine boy from Kentucky before he patrolled his beat in the Black Bottom, Paradise Valley area.

Three years after Turpin's appointment to this area, the Depression took hold and Paradise Valley was not unlike a strong heart in a decaying body. The residents of Black Bottom who previously felt the squeeze from poverty now felt the strangle-hold of depravation. This caused many to seek the only *equal opportunity employer* in town, *crime*. Bootleg liquor, prostitution, gambling, and policy houses were all lucrative businesses.

Where there is illegal activity, there are always rumors about "cops on the take." And although Ben Turpin had been dubbed with a number of names that are derogatory in nature, no one has ever spoke of him in this fashion. I assume then, that he must have been a person of some integrity no matter how warped his image may have appeared.

Ben Turpin earned only two demerits during his service of twenty-five years as a police officer. One of these was for shooting a Purple Gang hit man while off duty on October 14, 1929 at 11:30 p.m.. During this encounter, Turpin recognized a familiar face in the doorway of a Drug Store on Clairmount and St. Antoine. The man asked, "What the hell are you looking at?" Ben told him, using his *take-no-mess* language, "At you." When the man pulled out his gun, Ben pulled out his pearl handled revolver and

shot the Purple Gang member dead on the sidewalk. Turpin was charged with first degree murder, but a Recorder's Court jury, after deliberating only twenty minutes, acquitted him of the charges. In public, he received from his department a Meritorious Citation for "Exceptional Bravery."

"Turpin," Sgt. Glenn Walker who works in the Museum and Archives Department of the Detroit Police Department says, "was a legend of his time. He wasn't a bad person. He liked people. Anyone will tell you, he'd see people out in the street, they'd call him by name and he'd throw up his hand and wave. He just didn't take any mess — and he couldn't be bought."

From all accounts, Turpin's off duty time was spent pursuing his love of baseball and supporting the Turpin's Athletic Club, and still, he found the time to volunteer his supervision at the neighborhood theater. Another fact worth mentioning is that Turpin, who earned enough to afford better housing, elected to live in the neighborhood he had sworn to serve — sixty-square blocks of dilapidated housing called "Black Bottom." There are no verbal accounts of any other black officer who did so. Yet, Turpin was a visible part of this small-knit community where people sat on the front porch in the summer time and talked about each other's business while disciplining one-another's children.

Much is said of Ben Turpin's abuse of his own people, but despite the poverty and crime, Black Bottom residents respected the law and the families looked out for one another. There were no locked doors and windows and people called one another by name; and Henderson "Ben" Turpin was never — off-duty.

Truth expands and relaxes around the Ben Turpin legend depending on who is doing the talking. Still, many Detroiters, either from fear of reproach, or because of deep respect, wish to remain anonymous. One such source told me, "Turpin would have been an all-right person if he hadn't got addicted to Coke." Another claimed, "That man wasn't addicted to nothing, he was just a no good nigger who liked to beat up on people." A numbers runner who had used many aliases when he lived in Black Bottom and worked in and around Paradise Valley said, "If there were more Ben Turpins today, there wouldn't be so much crime."

When I lived in the Black Bottom area as a child, I was not allowed to go on Hastings Street. We lived only a block away on Palmer and St. Antoine, and Turpin's name was mentioned in whispers along with names like the Purple Gang. I had never any cause to fear him, but I did ruminate about the tales the adults told to the older children who tried to push the limits of curfew. Years ago, one such tale sent chills down my spine when I was being disciplined. My Uncle Lonnie said, "If Turpin catches any one of you children out after the sun goes down, he will bash your head in with his night stick. He carries a gun as well, and if he doesn't catch you to hit you with his night stick, he will shoot at you with his gun, and he is a good shot."

In those days, curfew was set by the family head and nearly always began just before dusk. Nearly forty-six-years after his patrol, Henderson "Ben" Turpin still lives as a legend in the minds of those who grew up in the thirties on the Eastside of Detroit and the Baby Boomer generation of Detroiters who experienced this form of discipline.

Richard Bak (Detroit Monthly/ April 1986) cites a number of instances in his writings on Turpin, but one account in particular lays a foundation of fact for my Uncle's depiction of Turpin's impartial heavy handed justice. Bak quotes Lieutenant Fred William's account of an incident between Ben Turpin and a woman at a ball park on Dequindre and Six mile on a Sunday afternoon in the early 1940s. The story goes — that a woman stepped on Turpin's foot. After she would not apologize, they got into a cursing match that ended with them wrestling in the aisles. Several stalwart men rushed to the woman's rescue, but hurried back to their own seats once they recognized Turpin, leaving the poor woman to fend for herself. Of course, there is the incident where Turpin reportedly struck Coleman Young's father in the mouth with his fist and threatened to beat him with his stick if he didn't keep his mouth shut. Old timers also say that Turpin killed at least twenty men. I have not, however, attempted to verify this claim. It is general knowledge that he wore a bullet-proof contraption that he fabricated under his coat and carried twin pearl handled pistols.

One could argue, too, that no one really knew Ben Turpin's private experiences and few knew his personal achievements. But, Turpin walked his beat in Detroit's black Ghetto during a period when the politics of killing blacks was acceptable in our country, and the fear of blacks as human beings saturated our society with integration laws. Toward the end of his life it is said that Ben Turpin was paranoid, and his behavior more erratic than ever. In death, his life and works remain to some extent inaccessible.

In 1952, Turpin retired from the Police Department, receiving the title of *Honorary Special Deputy*, the first time such an honor was bestowed. After retiring, Turpin worked as a hotel detective. In 1962, on August 8, Turpin, who had lost both legs to diabetes, died in Harper Hospital of a stroke. Fellow police officers helped to care for his wife until her death in the late seventies. They say he died and was buried without fanfare, shunned by the community he tried to serve the best way he knew how without benefit of all the high-tech training officers receive today.

Call it unassuming, but this writer feels that no other figure in East Detroit is more deserving of Black Detroit's appreciation and recognition than the rotund, human-gridlock dynamo called Ben Turpin.

Since then, Paradise Valley and Black Bottom have been wiped from the face of the earth, most of it in the late fifties and early sixties. Only a few old buildings remain and they are waiting for the wrecker's ball to make way for the new stadium complex. So... *where do we go from here????*

Sara

Oh, Sara did not plan
to be lonely.
But now, her years span a bit
past eighty-three.
Taking her last good stage bow
gracefully.
Time earlier,
Sara was like a bird, free.
All the townspeople knew her as
birdie, you see.
To enter her house, you didn't
need a key.
She was always in a
some-kind of hurry.
Whether helping derelicts or
little friends furry,
None of that caused
Sara to worry.
As we babes of the thirties
recollect,
One thing dear Sara
wants us to forget,
Her spicy midnight rambling,
getting all she could get.
Now that you ask,
Sara drags low.
Cats, dogs, birds, & kids are all
saddened, you know.
Because someone is taking Sara
away from here slow....

© 1994 Dwjuana J. Terrell

DETROIT INDEPENDENT

Guess Who? — Malcolm X at fifteen years old. *Courtesy of Jiam Desjardins Collection*

Nannie Geraldine Cox
(1933-1960)

by
Debraha Watson

Nannie Geraldine (Gerri) Cox made her way to Detroit from the coal mining town of Cinderella, West Virginia sometime during the early 50's. I'm not quite sure how she arrived, but I know she came seeking paradise. She had read about Paradise Valley and had saved several faded newspaper clippings that she treasured. She kept them neatly folded and wrapped in cellophane, tucked safely in a dingy-white beaded purse.

Gerri was a singer. Everybody back home said she was good. So it was to Detroit and the famous "Great Black Strip" that this nineteen-year-old country girl came to seek her fortune, and hopefully, to follow in the footsteps of such greats as Sarah Vaughan, Billie Holiday and Dinah Washington.

A young aspiring singer looking for her first big break, Gerri wandered the valley singing a few engagements here and there and partaking of the frenzied night life of the Garfield Lounge, Flame Show Bar, and other partying places. Although she tried for several years to make her mark while raising babies and working as a domestic, fate would not have it so. By the late 1950's, the strip had begun to fade, so had this Songbird's dreams.

Surrounded by decaying buildings and a weeping landscape, I'm told she stood on the corner of St.Antoine, deep in *The Valley*, and sang one last mournful song to an audience of ghosts.

A few years later, at the early age of twenty-seven, she died during the birth of her fourth child. Nannie was my *mother...*

Blues At Sunrise

Day break greets
red eyes,
dreams fade
discomfort.
Early news portrays
Jon Benet Ramsey's case
a farce.
Area school officials
take early buy outs,
Blacks continue
Black on Black crime.
Drunks piss
fermented grapes
in the middle of the street.
The only comfort
if comfort is the right word is,
Detroit is not the exception
to the rule
and love
does love somebody.

© 1997 Nathaniel Scott

Old Woman

You sit under a shelf
Of heavy brows and willows
Sun silvering your hair
Years bending your frame
No longer the tall, proud picture
of you
Your apron and calico dress
Unbuttoned at the neck
Your soft smock, big pocketed,
Just fit to hide fried apple-cakes
For your little "Jeannie"
Through your efforts,
Music criss-crossed
Many kitchen scenarios
You stand out
You flour-dusty baker
Gingerbread and apple turn-over
maker
A grown kid remembers
And music of those grand days
Do not disappear
In translation....

© 1984 Dwjuana Terrell

Pain

Do you ever wonder
why we cry?
It's because of all the pain
we hold inside.

Pain you can't see,
but you know it's there.
It's not on paper
or in the air.

You can hide it, fake it,
or try to keep strong.
But the pain you feel
is never, never
gone.

© 1997 Michanda Lynne Gant

DETROIT TIMES

WHAT'S LEFT?

NOT MUCH & TOMORROW THAT TOO

Paradise Valley Remembered

I close my eyes and visualize
a place of long ago.
A paradise which once thrived,
but now, it does not so.
Its streets, its businesses,
homes and people,
rated as high
as any steeple.
Paradise Valley stood alone,
when it came to places
on its own.
Paradise Valley, a spot of hope
if you were black.
A place where no one told you
to go to the back.
I feel the pride
within their hearts.
An essence of togetherness,
and not set apart.
I see Joe Louis
gracing its walls.
Joe Louis who helped lots of
men
to take their falls.
'Twas another Louis
who stood up tall,
Armstrong, first in jazz
and best overall.
Black Bottom, Jitterbug,
and Hully Gully, too.
Paradise's dance halls
opened nightly for you.
Coleman Young, Sonnie Wilson
and other notables as such,
all of them I can not name,
the number, it's just too much.
Ellington, Waller, Hampton,
and Calloway,
I hear them among its walls
even though they're gone away.

Paradise Valley,
its memory lives on.
Let us cherish it and keep it,
and never say, "So long."

© 1997 Shirley Green Haynes

SECTION VII — THE LEGACY

WILL BE GONE

VISIT THE MUSEUM OF AFRICAN-AMERICAN HISTORY AS OFTEN AS YOU CAN

Typical Brownstone on Brush *Courtesy of The Ernest Wimberly Collection*

Randora Hotel — 98 Garfield. The Garfield Lounge was in the basement.

House of Prostitution #1

June Bugs House *Courtesy of The Ernest Wimberly Collection*

Twelve Horsemen—First elite Black Social Club. Corner of Brush & Erskine

After Thought

Terror Of Living

Her strides on the
concrete are slow,
a deliberate beat
behind her own mutterings
life's defeat wrapped up
in a bag
hung low with other folks
cluttcrings

Her eyes never meet another's
her head will not turn
side to side
sudden stops at wire baskets
quick riffling through other's
trash
tag rag, the only thing
to break her stride

She does not see her judges
the owners of the discards
who tremble in fear of her mind
held in obsessive behavior
showing what it means to
survive

Incessant will
in the face of defeat
is shoddy transmogriflcation
thrown in a bag
She moves like an angel on
wings
hiding the "Haves" trash
in the form of things
disguised as a discarded hag

© 1997 Cheryl Wells

Massimo "Max"

He was the most generous
person I've known — my Dad.
Max was his name,
short for Massimo, the Greatest.
A gardener by trade,
he was an artist unsurpassed.
He could not turn away
from an outstretched hand
in need or want.
"Get a dish and another chair,"
was his frequent request
when anyone from the
neighborhood came to the door.
He was happiest when
they came at dinnertime.

Once, when I asked how rich
he would have been
had he kept it all.
He shrugged, "A millionaire,
but then look what
I would have missed."
He embodied the spirit of his
beloved mother
whose surname "Pacificio,"
fittingly means "Peace."

He died this year,
Two days after his beloved
Fourth of July
when flags are unfurled
under the hot July sun.
Family barbecues, flags,
and sparklers at dusk
Made him so very, very happy.

He didn't want to die,
This man of a magnanimous
heart,
But finally, he accepted
his death with courage
and grace.
God bless you, Dad.
Rest in Peace.

© 1994 Mary Ann Sestili

The First Sign of Snow

Each time we kissed,
I'd just tremble
No one ever made me
feel this way
And when we touched,
I'd get all limber
Why it had to end,
no one can say.

I cannot change
the stars in heaven
I am not the one
who lights the moon.
Were I the one,
I'd change the seasons
So summer would not leave us
quite so soon.

She was a fine feathered bird
I was one who loved her so
Yet, I knew that she would be
leaving me
Come the first sign of snow.

I cannot say
I did not know
Where within the scheme of
things
I stood
I just hoped
she'd stay around
When all the time
I knew she never would.

No, I won't say
I wasn't sorry
Sorry because
she could not stay
So I gave to her
my humble blessing
Kissed her hand
and watched her fly away.

She was a fine feathered bird
I was one who loved her so
Yet, I knew that she would be
leaving me
Come the first sign
of snow....

© 1984 Herbert R. Metoyer

Courtesy of The Ernest Wimberly Collection

SEVERAL RARE & UNUSUAL BUILDINGS

Courtesy of The Ernest Wimberly Collection

Courtesy of The Ernest Wimberly Collection

House of Prostitution #2

Carver Hotel on Canfield

Coleman Alexander Young 1918 - 1997
A Tuskegee Airman & Detroit's First Black Mayor
Paradise Valley was his stomping grounds

Accolades to Mayor Coleman A. Young

Thank you —for managing to momentarily distract us from the repetition of our daily lives by becoming the first African-American elected Mayor, of the city of Detroit.

Thank you — for paving the way for Sharon McPhail, Dennis Archer, John Conyers, Arthur Blackwell, and Charles Costa, for it is upon your shoulders that they stand.

Thank you — for rekindling hope out of the ashes of despair in a town that the media and politicians had declared dead.

Thank you — for the aggrandizement of the Mayoral Office because you stood firm, strong and confident in the face of adversity and controversy.

Thank you — for being an example to our children that they should not succumb to life's challenges nor to the small minds of mankind that will annihilate their dreams, but to be all that they can be.

Thank you — for remembering Black entrepreneurs and pulling them up the ladder of success along with you.

Thank you — for refusing to bow down to carefully orchestrated attacks on your character and administration that would have caused others to crumble.

Thank you — for allowing Kenneth Weiner and the FBI to prove that the best laid plans of both mice and men sometimes go wrong.

Thank you — for being able to stand against the wiles of the devil.

Thank you — for realizing that you are not perfect and reminding Bill Bonds that neither is he.

Thank you — for your "*mother wit*" and political savvy that left many news reporters speechless and in awe.

Thank you — Coleman Alexander Young, for taking time out of your life to give all that you had to give to the City of Detroit!

Thank you — for Being a Man. We THANK YOU, and we wish you well!

The Alpha House

THE OLD TIMERS

Jiam Desjardins (Skirv) Artist

Rarely does one encounter a multi-talented individual like Jiam. They are far and in between. An artist renown, he describes himself as a "Different Bag of Cats." I must agree. His artistic credentials are overwhelming. Somehow, he has managed to direct his diverse talents into active careers on both coasts as an artist/illustrator, as well as an actor, writer, producer and director in radio, television, films, and stage. He also produces music videos.

Born and raised in "Paradise Valley," Jiam is also a historian of some notoriety and served as advisor to the staff in the preparation of this book. When he is not tied down, he travels the world over, collecting antiques, unusual artifacts, and other collectibles.

TAKE PRIDE IN WHAT YOU —ALREADY HAVE— NURTURE IT & IT WILL GROW

Polly Johnson, Head of the Polly Johnson Cancer Foundation & 1st Queen of Paradise Valley

The Final Tribute
An Ode To Ted

Briefly in my life
there glowed a star
A welcoming beacon
whether near or far

This happens in the lives
of a precious few
Just those whose lives
were touched by you

Now my shining star,
you're gone away
But I know your soul's
with God today

I ask God to let it be
That someday I will dwell with thee
United in heaven as one brilliant star
Glowing brightly from afar.

© 1997 Jewel Martin

Bill Murray — Former Mo-Town Producer turned Screen Actor

Ember

'neath the fragile pale of skin
lies heat not even Satan's seen
passion packaged pure so tight
that I'm asbestos-man in fright
when your lips caress my name
I'm blasted by the solar flames
wind-tunneling across my soul
like some brave martyr
God took whole
beaten by the forger's sledge
with quickened quench
and fine-honed edge
so I emerge from chrysalis
to drink your little smile of bliss
now 'round your head
spin ringed planets small
these words of love
that hold us both enthralled

© 1997 Marc Maurus

DON'T YOU WISH WE COULD BUY IT BACK?

PARADISE VALLEY / BLACK BOTTOM

Unknown Singer at The Rhinoceros with Sunnie Wilson & Debraha Watson

DID YOU SELL YOURS TOO?

Herb Metoyer & Barbara Rose Collins
New Year's Eve 1998

DETROIT BLACK WRITER'S GUILD

Gerri Metoyer, Sonnie Wilson, & Debraha Watson

Jiam DesJardines poses in front of the house he grew up in.

Barbara Rose Collins & Polly Johnson
New Year's Eve 1998

– ACKNOWLEDGMENTS –

There are many persons we would like to thank. For without them, the success of this project would have been seriously handicapped.

The following persons, however, contributed tangible and/or financial resources toward the production of this work. They have, therefore, been dubbed as esteemed "Patrons of The Guild" and are deserving of Special Recognition.

Alexander Jefferson (Detroit, MI)
Alpha Kappa Alpha Sorority (Detroit, MI)
Alpha Phi Alpha Fraternity (Detroit, MI)
Apple BookStore (Detroit, MI)
Barbara Pattee (Detroit, MI)
Barbara Rose Collins (Detroit, MI)
Burton Historical Library - Detroit Public Library (Detroit, MI)
Carmen Brown (Detroit, MI)
Debraha Watson (Detroit, MI)
Delores McFarland (Southfield, MI)
Denise Beauregard (Detroit, MI)
Donald Robinson (Detroit, MI)
Dr. Anthony Rene & Dr. Mary Ann Sestili (Potomac, MD)
Dr. Barbara Ann Woodson (Southfield, MI)
Dr. Noah Levy Family Dentistry (Southfield, MI)
Dr. Edward & Rose Emma Franklin (Columbia, MD)
Evelyn Holmes (Allen Park, MI)
Evelyn Rhodes (Detroit, MI)
George Moore & Family (Detroit, MI)
George Ramsey & Lenard Shannon, Collaborative Learning LLC (Detroit, MI)
Herbert & Geraldine Metoyer (Southfield, MI)
James N. Ware (Detroit, MI)
John Engel - LUTCF, John Hancock Financial Services, Lakeside Agency (Sterling Hts. MI)
Joseph Claiborne (Detroit, MI)
Kieth Dye, City View Newspaper, (Detroit, MI)
Kimani Jones (Detroit, MI)
Leroy & Jacqueline Caffey (Detroit, MI)
Marie A. Berry (Southfield, MI)
Michael & Faye Terry (Hinesville, GA)
Michael Goodin, Michigan Chronicle (Detroit, MI)
Michigan Council for Arts and Cultural Affairs (Detroit, MI)
Mildred Jackson (Oakdale, LA)
Patrick Moore (Detroit, MI)
Reginald Larrie, (Detroit, MI)
Robert J. Haynes (Inkster, MI)
Robert Jones (Detroit, MI)
Sandra Miller (Detroit, MI)
Southern University Alumni (Detroit, MI)
Steve's Soul Food (Detroit, MI)
Teresa Kimble (Detroit, MI)
William & Delores Metoyer-Finister (Gaithersburg, MD)

Index of Authors

Photographs Indexed By Donor

Portrait of Beauty

i'm told my vision is blurred
by the fairy tales of my youth
for only in such worlds
can imagination exist
they say it's until tomorrow
as they chuckle their inner
wombs
i fear they once knew it, too
before the bitterness of age
perhaps they saw a replica
the picture i voiced to their ears
and maybe, they'll remember
if i repeat it again

its frame is carved with details
showing the masculine of
baroque
each corner socket, a limb for
the body
to hold the form and preserve
the work
the touch feels of smooth silk
such a magnetic bond
a delight for hands to polish
until it shines like pure gold

the canvas is toned in black
no tan, yellow, beige, or white
just generations of darkness
revealing chains and severed
roots
i love when it's there before me
as i look to receive its pleasures
it stares back to give that in
which i came
for me and me only

someday, i hope to meet its
creator
an artist of fine craftsmanship
i know this work was made for
me
it conveys all my sensual emo-
tions
to learn such an authentic skill
i'll repaint its embodied shell
with tongue shall I trace the
outer form
so every part i'll know
and having its mark in my
inner soul
i can produce a carbon of my
view
but it will not be the work of
its painter
the new birth will have traits
of me

then, one day, i will tell my
female child
about the portrait of beauty i
know
i'll raise her around the frame
that's mine
and teach her what i speak is
truly so....

Retrospect

High in the heavens
From nowhere and yet,
from somewhere,
A lonely drop of rain forms
Gathering substance
It slips from its lofty perch
To ride the angry wind
Wondering how it started
Knowing how it ends.
Driven ever downward
It struggles against the tide
Until, at last,
It splatters
Upon the thirsty earth
There in retrospect to reside
Awaiting nature's call,
To repeat again, and again,
Its quite spectacular fall.
But that particular rain drop
As it was, in all its uniqueness,
Will never be again.
Instead, it will be
An infinitesimal part
Of another whole,
And the whole of, yet,
Another magic part....